TOP 10
MEXICO CITY

NANCY MIKULA

DK

EYEWITNESS TRAVEL

Left **Voladores, Museo Nacional de Antropología** Right **Catedral Metropolitana**

Contents

DK

LONDON, NEW YORK,
MELBOURNE, MUNICH AND DELHI
www.dk.com

Printed and bound in China

First American Edition, 2008

15 10 9 8 7 6 5 4

Published in the United States by
DK Publishing, 345 Hudson Street
New York, New York, 10014

Reprinted with revisions 2010, 2012

A catalog record for this book is available
from the Library of Congress

ISSN 1479-344X
ISBN 978-0-7566-8542-3

Within each Top 10 list in this book,
no hierarchy of quality or popularity is
implied. All 10 are, in the editor's opinion,
of roughly equal merit.

MIX
Paper from
responsible sources
FSC™ C018179
www.fsc.org

Mexico City's Top 10

Left **Cantina, Coyoacán** Right **Interior, Capilla del Cerrito, Villa de Guadalupe**

Left **Gardens, Castillo de Chapultepec** Right **Museo Frida Kahlo**

 Key to abbreviations
Adm *admission charge payable*

3

MEXICO CITY'S TOP 10

MEXICO CITY'S TOP 10

Mexico City's Highlights

Pulsating with life and culture, blessed with perpetually spring-like weather, and with a fascinating blend of history and modernity, Mexico City is endlessly surprising. With excellent museums, ornate churches, colonial palaces, and urban parks, the city attracts a large number of visitors.

Museo Nacional de Antropología
One of the great museums of the world dramatically presents its pre-eminent collection of Mexican pre-Hispanic art by region *(see pp8–11).*

Catedral Metropolitana
The largest and most important colonial cathedral in the Western Hemisphere, it took almost three centuries to build and majestically blends Baroque and Neo-Classical styles *(see pp12–13).*

Palacio Nacional
This massive executive palace and government office stands along the east side of the Zócalo and showcases Diego Rivera's famous mural, *Epic of the Mexican People (see pp14–15).*

DEPORTIVO REYN

Vallejo

Naucalpan

Nue
Santa Ma

Museo Nacion
de Antropolog 1

Lomas

Bosque de 6 ME
Chapultepec

CONSTITUYENTES

Del Valle

Santa Fé

San Mateo
Tlalltenango

Coyoacá

San
Ángel

San
Jerónimo   El Pedreg

ANILLO PERIFÉRICO

Cuarto
Dinamo   Tlalpan

San Miguel
Ajusco

Parque Nacional
los Dinamos

2 ⎯⎯ miles ⎯ 0 ⎯ km ⎯⎯ 2

Templo Mayor
An accidental discovery led to a massive archeological effort that uncovered the ruins of this Aztec temple. A museum was built to house the artifacts recovered *(see pp16–17).*

Palacio de Bellas Artes
The spectacular performing arts *palacio* is a city icon, combining an exquisite white marble exterior with an Art Deco interior having Mexican touches *(see pp20–21).*

Preceding pages Main altar, Ex-Convento e Iglesia del Carmen, San Ángel

Centro Histórico

Bosque de Chapultepec
Mexico City's lovely urban park is one of the largest in the world and home to many of the city's top museums and family attractions *(see pp22–5)*.

Museo Nacional de Arte
This exquisite *palacio* is home to the nation's extensive art collection, encompassing nearly five centuries of magnificent masterpieces by Mexico's finest artists, including Miguel Cabrera, José María Velasco, Diego Rivera, and many others *(see pp26–7)*.

Xochimilco Floating Gardens
Colorfully decorated *trajineras* (flat barges), propelled by boatmen with long poles, carry merry-makers on floating-parties along the shady, tree-lined Aztec canals of Xochimilco, "the place where flowers grow" *(see pp28–9)*.

Villa de Guadalupe
One of the holiest Catholic shrines in the Western Hemisphere honors the Virgin de Guadalupe, Mexico's patron saint, who appeared in a vision to an indigenous Mexican peasant, Juan Diego in 1531 *(see pp30–31)*.

Teotihuacán
The largest archeological site in Mesoamerica, and one of the most impressive in the world, this ancient city reached its zenith in AD 550 *(see pp32–5)*.

🔟 Museo Nacional de Antropología

One of the most important of its kind in the world, this anthropological museum presents an outstanding collection of Mexican pre-Hispanic art in a stunning modern building. A dramatic central courtyard, highlighted by a spectacular fountain, is surrounded by a series of halls, each showcasing an ancient Mexican culture and society.

Carved pillar and water fountain

Cacaxtla fresco paintings

⭐ Arrive early in the morning to avoid the worst of the daily crowds. If you have limited time, visit the Mexica Hall first to see the fabulous Aztec collection.

🍴 The café downstairs is excellent, offering a full lunch buffet as well as sandwiches, salads, and full meals.

- Map E3
- Avenida Paseo de la Reforma, and Calzada Gandhi, in Colonia Chapultepec
- 5553-6381
- Metro 7 Auditorio and Metro 1 Chapultepec, Turibus Centro stop #17
- 9am–7pm Tue–Sun
- 51 pesos. Children, students, teachers, seniors over 60 free with appropriate ID. Free Sun for Mexican citizens and residents
- Audioguides available
- www.mna.inah.gob.mx

Top 10 Features

1. Pre-Classic Central Mexico Hall
2. Teotihuacán Hall
3. Toltec Hall
4. Aztec or Mexica Hall
5. Oaxaca Hall
6. Gulf Coast Hall
7. Maya Hall
8. Western Cultures Hall
9. Northern Cultures Hall
10. Ethnography Halls

Key

▮ First Floor
▮ Second Floor

1 Pre-Classic Central Mexico Hall

The hall features artifacts that highlight the achievements in pottery and stone sculpture during the years 2300 BC to AD 100. The Acrobat from Tlatilco, a fine vase, is displayed here.

2 Teotihuacán Hall

The finely crafted artistic, religious, and architectural objects displayed in the hall *(above)* reflect the skills of the craftsmen, artisans, and builders of this first great Mexican city. The craftsmen depicted deities in stone carvings, finely painted murals, and on intricately decorated vessels. The huge monolith of the goddess Chalchiuhtlicue is one of the highlights of the hall.

➲ *Designed by Pedro Ramírez Vázquez and completed in 1964, the two-story museum encloses 474,000 sq ft (44,000 sq m) of space*

Toltec Hall
This hall displays art objects from the great Toltec city-states that developed from 850–1250. The sculpture of a bearded warrior emerging from the mouth of a coyote *(above)* can be seen here.

Aztec or Mexica Hall
The museum's largest hall is filled with impressive monoliths and finely crafted objects representative of the immense diversity of Aztec culture. The centerpiece is the intricately carved Sun Stone, a circular disk representing the Mexica cosmos *(see p10)*.

Oaxaca Hall
This hall showcases artifacts from the two cultures that flourished in Oaxaca – Zapotec and Mixtec. There is a reconstruction of the Zapotec Tomb of Monte Albán and many elegant clay vessels with various figures on them. The Mixtec collection features silver and gold pieces, and carved jade and obsidian.

Gulf Coast Hall
The Olmecs are known for the colossal stone head sculptures of their leaders *(above)*, two of which are in this hall. Also displayed are stone masks and sculptures.

Maya Hall
Exquisite examples of highly decorated temple architecture and fine artistic creations of Mayan civilization fill the hall. There are also many stucco figures that illustrate the Mayan ideal of human beauty.

Western Cultures Hall
This hall displays artifacts from western Mexico, including pottery figurines and vessels of unusual complexity and fine design. The hunchbacked figure of a god on a serpent is notable.

Northern Cultures Hall
The hall features artifacts from northern Mexico. Pottery, masks, and weapons form the largest portion of the collection. The highlight is the finely formed decorated pottery from Paquimé featuring red or black designs on cream-colored vessels.

Ethnography Halls
The second floor of the museum is filled with brilliantly colored textiles, costumes, and art of the indigenous people from all regions of Mexico. Cultures are organized by state and in relation to the anthropology halls downstairs.

Museum Guide
The entrance hall contains the gift shop, restrooms, temporary exhibit rooms, and ticket area. It opens into a huge courtyard whose roof is supported by a modern carved pillar and water fountain. The courtyard has doors that open into the museum halls. Each of the halls displays archeological objects from a different region or culture in Mexico and each has a door that leads into an exterior garden area where reconstructions and artifacts are on show. The entire upper floor showcases the ethnology collection.

In the garden of the Maya Hall is a reconstruction of Palenque's Temple of Inscriptions

Left **Model of Tenochtitlán's Sacred Center** Right **Aztec stone head**

Aztec or Mexica Hall

Sun Stone

1 This magnificent monolith depicts the first four Aztec worlds, thought to represent locations where the Aztecs lived before relocating to Tenochtitlán in 1323. The central figure is either the sun god or the earth god, with a sacrificial knife for a tongue, and claws holding human hearts. The four squares surrounding the center depict the four previous worlds, represented by a jaguar, wind, fiery rain, and water. The next circle of twenty squares represents the Aztec month made up of 20 days. Other symbols depict the 18 months of a year and five sacrifice days, representing the 365 days of the Aztec year.

Sun Stone

Coatlicue

2 Several monumental sculptures of Coatlicue, the mother goddess, who gave birth to the sun, moon, and stars survive. One sculpture reveals her deadly side, with a head like a snake, a necklace of human hands and hearts, and a skirt of serpents.

Tenochtitlán and Tlatelolco

3 A beautiful painting by Luis Covarrubias (1919–87) presents an idealized view of the shimmering lake-cities of Tenochtitlán and Tlatelolco before the conquest, based on written descriptions by Cortés and other Spaniards. Although Templo Mayor is shown larger than it was, the painting offers a stunning glimpse of the lost cities.

Obsidian Monkey Vessel

4 One of the museum's most valuable and most viewed objects, this charming vessel in the form of a monkey holding its tail in both hands is carved from a single piece of highly polished obsidian. The monkey, in Aztec mythology, is associated with the god of wind and black rain clouds.

Headdress of Quetzal Feathers

5 The headdress on display is a replica of the original which Moctezuma II presented to Cortés. A complete arc of elegant turquoise quetzal feathers are mounted on an exquisite headband decorated with red beads, turquoise, and gold.

Coyolxauhqui

6 The huge stone head of Coyolxauhqui, goddess of the moon, depicts her warrior goddess persona. Her cheeks are decorated with rattlesnakes. According to Aztec myth, she was beheaded by her brother, Huitzilopochtli – the sun god – for impeding his birth.

7 Cuauhxicalli of Moctezuma I

Moctezuma I, the fifth Aztec emperor, consolidated the empire. His military victories are displayed on this enormous, intricately carved, wheel-shaped stone. Eleven historical conquest scenes are depicted, showing battles that occurred in different parts of Mexico.

8 Xochipilli

The god of music, song, flowers, and love, Xochipilli sits on his throne decorated with butterflies and flowers, the symbols of his realm.

9 Ocelotl-Cuauhxicalli

A *cuauhxicalli* is a type of altar stone and is used to conduct sacrifices to the gods. The eagle and jaguar are common animal motifs used. *Ocelotl* is the Aztec name for a jaguar.

10 Chapulín

This unusual, large, red-colored stone grasshopper, or *chapulín*, was found on Cerro del Chapulín, Grasshopper Hill, which is the hill in Bosque de Chapultepec *(see pp22–3)* that the Castillo stands on today. This place was sacred to the Aztecs and they built a temple here.

Top 10 Aztec Deities

1. Huitzilopochtli, supreme god of sun and war
2. Coyolxauhqui, goddess of the moon
3. Quetzalcoatl, god of wind and fertility
4. Tezcatlipoca, god of night, discord, and sorcerers
5. Xochipilli, god of love, beauty, dance, and flowers
6. Mixcoatl, god of hunting and the Milky Way
7. Ometeotl, lord of duality
8. Xiuhtecutli, god of fire and lord of turquoise
9. Tlaloc, god of rain and fertility
10. Coatlicue, goddess who birthed the sun god Huitzilopochtli, the moon, and stars

Aztec relief sculpture of the birth of Quetzalcoatl

Mythology

The Aztecs believed that the world was created by the gods, and that their world was in the fifth and final iteration – the Sun Stone, the monolithic centerpiece of the Aztec Hall, is believed to depict the first four worlds. The heavens were comprised of vertical levels, with the supreme creators, the gods, reigning in the top level. Among the gods, one of the most important was Coatlicue, an Earth goddess who gave birth to the sun, moon, and stars. Another creation myth describes the formation of the world by rival twins, Quetzalcoatl and Tezcatlipoca, representing good and evil. Aztec mythology held that the Universe is comprised of four parts, corresponding to the four cardinal directions with the convergence ruled from the center by Xiuhtecutli, god of fire and lord of turquoise. The reason that there are often multiple myths explaining single aspects of belief is that the Aztecs borrowed heavily from the Toltec, Teotihuacán, and other cultures. It is estimated that the Aztecs had a pantheon of over 1,500 deities when the Spanish, under the leadership of Cortés, arrrived in 1519.

Coatlicue, the mother goddess

Catedral Metropolitana

With its richly ornate Spanish Baroque façade, Neo-Classical dome, and twin bell towers rising 220 ft (67 m), the cathedral is a majestic blend of architectural styles. Begun in 1525 it was designed and built in stages by many architects, artists, and sculptors. The cathedral was consecrated in 1667 and completed in 1813.

Altar of Forgiveness, Catedral Metropolitana

⊘ The Altar of Forgiveness and several side chapels are always accessible, but the rest of the cathedral is restricted during mass.

The exterior of the cathedral is most beautiful in the early evening when the lights are on and it glows against the twilight sky.

Look through the glass panels under your feet in the courtyard to see the original courtyard and steps.

🅾 The rooftop restaurant of the Majestic Hotel offers views of the Catedral Metropolitana from across the Zócalo.

- Map Q2
- Zócalo
- Metro Zócalo
- 8am–8pm daily
- Free

Top 10 Features

1. Pendulum
2. Capilla de San José
3. Pipe Organs and Choir Loft
4. Capilla de San Felipe de Jesús
5. Altar del Perdón
6. Altar de los Reyes
7. Pinnacle
8. Metropolitana Sacrarium
9. Miguel Cabrera Masterpieces
10. Capilla de Nuestra Señora de los Dolores

Pendulum
For years the cathedral had been sinking into the soft soil of what was once a lake. Extensive underground engineering efforts have largely stabilized the building. The pendulum *(above)* suspended from the ceiling tracks the tilt, marking a record on the floor.

Capilla de San José
This side chapel along the west wall of the cathedral can be easily recognized by the colorful ribbons placed in front of the statue of Saint Ramon. The devout believe that a woman can leave a ribbon inscribed with a personal message and a lock to put a stop to gossip doing the rounds in the village.

Choir, Catedral Metropolitana

Pipe Organs and Choir Loft
Two magnificent pipe organs *(below)* flank a huge two-level choir loft which has intricately worked stalls. Carved figures of bishops and saints decorate the upper level; ivory figures adorn the center.

4 Capilla de San Felipe de Jesús

Dedicated in 1636, this chapel *(right)* honors San Felipe de Jesús, the first Mexican Saint. The 17th-century paintings illustrate scenes from his life. The urn on the right side of the chapel contains the remains of Don Agustin de Iturbe, the first Mexican ruler following independence from Spain.

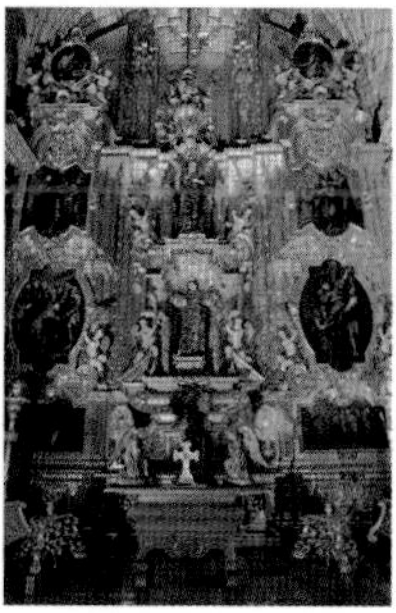

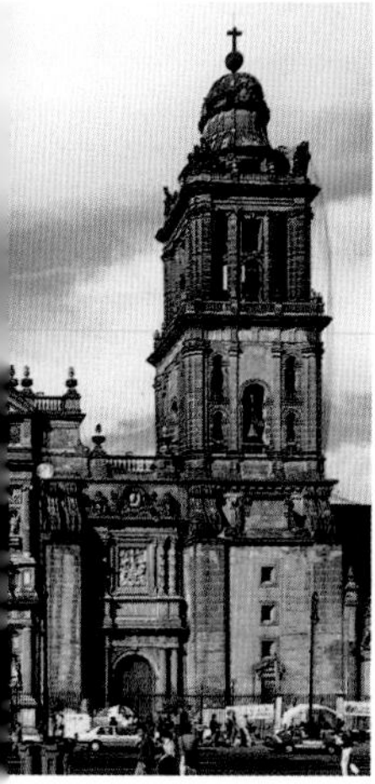

5 Altar del Perdón

This splendid gold altar, created by Jerónimo de Balbás, stands behind the Doors of Forgiveness, the central entrance to the cathedral from the Zócalo. The doors are open only on special occasions.

6 Altar de los Reyes

This Baroque masterpiece *(right)* by sculptor Jerónimo de Balbás is dedicated to canonized Kings and Queens. The altar has the paintings *Adoration of the Kings* and *Assumption of the Virgin* both by Juan Rodríguez Juárez.

7 Pinnacle

Sculptures of the three virtues, Faith, Hope, and Charity, adorn the pinnacle of the clock tower designed by Spanish architect Manuel Tolsá and completed in 1813. Tolsá was the cathedral's final architect, and was responsible for adding many of the details that harmonized and unified the completed design.

8 Metropolitana Sacrarium

The sculpted façade of this parish church, which is attached to the cathedral, is considered to be the foremost example of the Churrigueresque style in Mexico. Built by Spaniard Lorenzo Rodríquez from 1740–68, the interior is in the Moorish style.

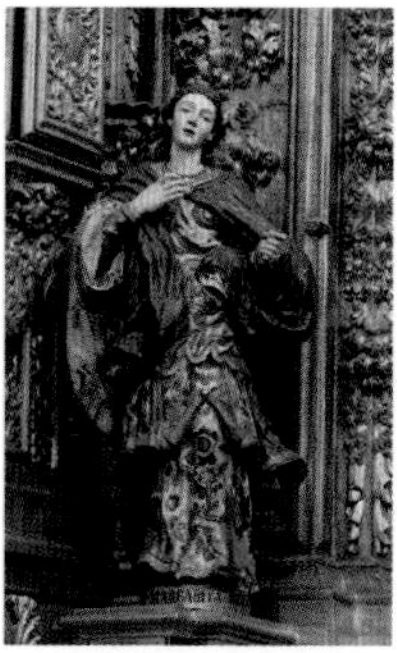

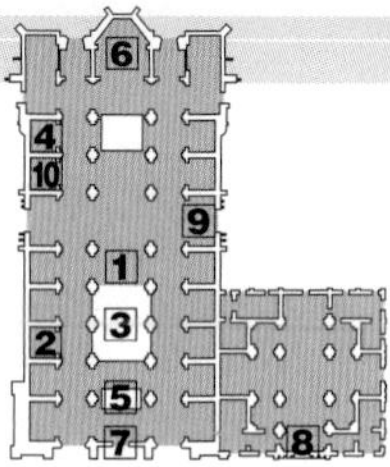

9 Miguel Cabrera Masterpieces

Four spectacular masterpieces by Oaxaca painter Miguel Cabrera hang in the vestibules above the cathedral's side doors *(below)*.

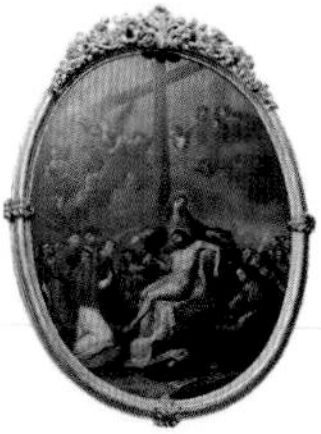

10 Capilla de Nuestra Señora de los Dolores

The oldest chapel in the cathedral, it was completed around 1600. The image of Nuestra Señora de los Dolores in the center of the main altar is by Clemente Terrazas.

Cathedral Guide

Enter from the courtyard on the north side of the Zócalo. In the front center, is the Altar del Perdón. Behind this altar are the choir loft and two pipe organs. Next is the main altar with the Altar de los Reyes at the rear of the cathedral. There are seven chapels along the left and right side of the cathedral and at its center, between the choir loft and the main altar, hangs the pendulum that measures the tilt of the building.

The cathedral was built on the site of an Aztec temple

🔟 Palacio Nacional

This enormous palace dominates the entire east side of the Zócalo. Aztec Emperor Moctezuma II's castle stood here before Cortés destroyed it and constructed his own. The building has been expanded several times, and today it is used by the Mexican Government. The impressive edifice is made of granite and tezontle, a red stone.

Staircase of the Empress, Palacio Nacional

📷 Have your photo ID available when you enter the door; the guards are efficient and may look in large bags.

💬 The rooftop restaurant of the Hotel Majestic *(see p113)* offers excellent views of the Zócalo and is the perfect place to eat breakfast and watch the flag hoisting ceremony.

- Map Q3
- Zócalo
- 3688-1261
- Metro Zócalo
- 8am–6pm daily
- Free
- Photo ID required for admittance
- Guided tours
- www.palacionacional mexico.com

Top 10 Features

1. Façade
2. Epic of the Mexican People
3. Historical Murals by Diego Rivera
4. Independence Bell
5. Benito Juárez Museo
6. Garden Patio
7. Pegasus Fountain
8. Staircase of the Empress
9. Presidential Balcony
10. Flag Ceremony

Façade
Three doors provide access to the impressive interior of this executive palace. The door on the right is for diplomatic access only and is also the door used by the President of Mexico. The door to the left was formerly used by the Finance Department and was dreaded by all who had to enter to settle their taxes. The central door is the main entrance and leads into a grand central courtyard.

Epic of the Mexican People
Diego Rivera painted his exquisitely colorful and detailed masterpiece on the walls of the central staircase from 1925–35. It provides an incredibly rich and vibrant visual history of the Mexican people from pre-Hispanic times through the Mexican Revolution. Full of life and whimsy, the mural captures the very essence of the nation.

Pegasus Fountain, Palacio Nacional

Historical Murals by Diego Rivera
The second floor hallway has nine murals by Rivera painted from 1941–52. Eight portray idealized views of village life before Cortés came. The ninth shows a village after Cortés' arrival.

Independence Bell
Padre Miguel Hidalgo rang this bell *(above)* in 1810, when he called for Mexican Independence. The bell was moved here in 1896 by Porfirio Díaz.

There is a tradition of ringing the Independence Bell every September 15th, Mexican Independence Day

Pegasus Fountain
The beautiful main courtyard inside the palace features a lovely fountain with a statue of Pegasus, the Greek winged horse. Government functions are held here.

Benito Juárez Museo
The President's office, bedroom, dining room, parlor, and other interesting memorabilia from his time in office are featured in this museum *(above)*.

Staircase of the Empress
This simple but elegant staircase with its ornate brass railings has only two flights of stairs and no visible support.

Flag Ceremony
With impressive pomp and ceremony a large Mexican honor guard marches out of the Palacio Nacional each morning and crosses the street to the Zócalo where they raise an enormous Mexican flag *(below)*. All the hustle and bustle in the plaza halts as the flag is raised in a formal drill. The ceremony is repeated every evening when the huge flag is lowered.

Garden Patio
A delightful botanical garden *(below)* lies secluded in the inner courtyard at the back of the palace just beyond the entrance to the Benito Juárez Museo. It is quiet, peaceful, and sheltered from traffic noise. Walk the geometrically placed, paved garden paths or sit on a shady bench and enjoy one of the city's prettiest gardens.

Presidential Balcony
On Mexican Independence Day, September 15th, the president of Mexico stands on this balcony *(above)* just above the central door of the palace and repeats Padre Miguel Hidalgo's famous call for Independence *(see p38)*. Thousands of spectators gather on the Zócalo to witness the event.

Site Guide
Enter through the central door and turn left. The staircase with the Diego Rivera murals is on your left. Walk up the stairs, the murals are on the walls above the landing. Continue up the stairs to the second floor and turn left to see the historical murals. Return to the first floor and turn left to visit the Staircase of the Empress, the Benito Juárez Museo, and the Garden Patio. Walk through the garden and re-enter the palace. Cross the main courtyard and come back out through the front door.

Templo Mayor

In Aztec times the Templo Mayor stood in a sacred walled compound in the center of Tenochtitlán (present day Mexico City) before Cortés destroyed it. In 1978 a massive round carved stone was uncovered accidentally near Zócalo that led to a major archeological project, uncovering the ruins of the magnificent double pyramid complex.

Model of the temple and its construction stages

⭐ Early morning (or a cloudy day) is the best time to visit the ruins, before the sun's glare makes it difficult to see the details of sculptures and murals.

🍽 Bypass the street food around Templo Mayor and head to one of the hotels along the south side of Zócalo, or head farther south along Francisco I. Madero to #29 and stop in at Los Bisquets Obregón.

- Map Q2
- Seminario 8, on the east side of the Catedral Metropolitana
- 4040-5600
- Metro Zócalo
- 9am–5pm Tue–Sun
- 51 pesos, free Sun for Mexican citizens and residents, free for children (under 13), students, and teachers
- Audio guides (Spanish and English); additional fee for video cameras
- www.templomayor. inah.gob.mx

Top 10 Features

1. Museo del Templo Mayor
2. Lacustrine Fountain
3. Monolith of Coyolxauhqui
4. Wall of Skulls
5. Chacmool Carving
6. Eagle Knights
7. Templo Mayor Construction Stages
8. Temple of Tláloc
9. Serpent Head Sculptures
10. Tenochtitlán Ceremonial Center

Museo del Templo Mayor

This museum designed by Mexican architect Pedro Ramírez Vázquez displays many of the artifacts discovered during the excavation of the temple ruins, including the original monolith of Coyolxauhqui.

Lacustrine Fountain

An excellent fountain-cum-map *(above)* is located in the plaza. The base of the fountain forms a bas-relief map of ancient Tenochtitlán surrounded by the lake, canals, irrigation ditches, and small islands. This provides a contextual overview of the city that surrounded Templo Mayor before the Spanish conquest.

Monolith of Coyolxauhqui

This magnificent circular carved stone *(above)* depicts the dismembered Coyolxauhqui, goddess of the moon.

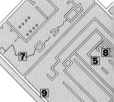

Wall of Skulls

During the Aztec times skulls of sacrificed prisoners were mounted on wooden stakes forming a wall of skulls *(below)*, or a *Tzompantli*. The Wall of Skulls found in the museum is a replica of the original. In the ruins, there is also a wall of stucco-covered human skulls that forms a side wall of the Tzompantli Altar.

➤ *The 20-minute video in the museum, near the entrance, is excellent*

Chacmool Carving

This polychrome sculpted figure *(above)* in a reclining pose cradles a bowl on its belly which was used to hold peaceful offerings to Tláloc.

7 Templo Mayor Construction Stages

The Templo Mayor was enlarged seven times as the stature and prosperity of the Aztecs increased. These enlargements, referred to as construction stages, can be seen on a walk through the ruins *(right)*.

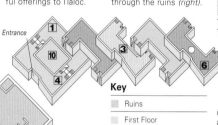

Key

▓	Ruins
▓	First Floor
▓	Second Floor
▓	Third Floor
▓	Fourth Floor
▓	Fifth Floor

8 Temple of Tláloc

The Aztecs made peaceful offerings to the Chacmool sculpture in the Temple of Tláloc, god of rain, to ensure successful harvests, fertility, and abundance.

9 Serpent Head Sculptures

Intricately carved and brightly painted stone serpent heads *(above)* are seen to guard the base of the main staircase of this great Aztec temple.

6 Eagle Knights

Two of these remarkable life-size clay sculptures, each comprising five interlocking parts, were discovered in the House of the Eagles near the temple. One of them is on display in the museum *(above)*. The Eagle Knights were elite Aztec warriors who dressed as birds of prey.

10 Tenochtitlán Ceremonial Center

This large scale model of Templo Mayor surrounded by other buildings in the ceremonial center of Tenochtitlán creates a powerful visual contrast to the Spanish colonial buildings standing in the city center. The imposing architecture of the temple and the city of Tenochtitlán were so impressive that the early Spanish colonizers compared it to the great cities of Europe.

Site Guide

Look at the fountain near the entrance which depicts the pre-Hispanic Aztec city of ancient Tenochtitlán. Turn left as you enter the gate and follow the one-way outdoor walkway through the ruins. At the far end of the ruins the path ends at the museum entrance. Look at the model of the Tenochtitlán Ceremonial Center as it would have once stood, and then visit the eight museum rooms in sequence. Turn right at the museum entrance, watch the video before proceeding up the stairs to room 1. Continue through rooms 2, 3, 4, and 5. Rooms 4 and 5 are interconnected. Finally take the stairs back down to rooms 6, 7, and 8.

Templo Mayor was a symbolic representation of an Aztec sacred mythical place, Coatepec or "the Hill of the Serpent"

🔟 Palacio de Bellas Artes

A true masterpiece of architectural design, the lovely Palacio de Bellas Artes is one of Mexico City's most beloved buildings and is home to an excellent performing arts center. It was designed by Italian architect Adamo Boari. Its broad plaza and formal flower gardens blend into the natural beauty of the adjacent Alameda Central.

Sculpture, central lunette, Palacio de Bellas Artes

🕐 Admission is free on Sundays; the theater is open to the public (1–1:30pm Mon–Fri and during events).

There is an extra charge to visit the Museo Nacional de Arquitectura, of most interest to serious architecture fans.

🍴 Dine surrounded by resplendent Art Deco at the Café del Palacio in the lobby.

- Map N2
- Eje Central Lázaro Cárdenas and Av Juárez
- 5512-2593
- 10am–5:30pm Tue–Sun
- 39 pesos, free Sun, free for students, and teachers
- www.bellasartes. gob.mx

Top 10 Features

1. Statues of Pegasus
2. Façade Sculptures
3. Eagle
4. Lobby and Vestibule
5. Courtyard
6. Murals
7. Theater
8. Art Exhibitions
9. Museo Nacional de Arquitectura
10. Ballet Folklórico de México

Statues of Pegasus
Four sculptures of the winged horse, Pegasus, in a variety of aspects, by Agustín Querol, stand in the esplanade in front of the entrance to the performing arts center *(below)*.

Façade Sculptures
The exterior façade has intricate and ornate sculptures in the arch above the main doorway. In the center, Leonardo Bistolfi's (1859–1933) *Birth of Venus* represents harmony. The statues on either side, by Boni, symbolize love and hate.

Lobby and Vestibule
A classic Art Deco black marble stairway, leads into the vestibule. Across the black-and-white marble floor are the metallic theater doors *(below)*.

Eagle
On the dome is Geza Marotti's sculpture of the Mexican national symbol, an eagle *(below)*. It is perched on a cactus, eating a snake. Figures under the eagle represent comedy, tragedy, drama, and lyrical drama.

 Preceding pages **Aerial view of Palacio de Bellas Artes at dusk**

Courtyard
⑤ The four-story courtyard is light, airy, and dramatic with red marble columns and a high, four-domed ceiling (above).

Murals
⑥ Famous muralists Rufino Tamayo, Diego Rivera, David Alfaro Siqueiros, and José Clemente Orozco painted their huge murals on the walls of the second and third floors of the building facing the courtyard. The contrast between the traditional Art Deco interior and the political murals painted with unusually bright colors heightens the dramatic tone in the space.

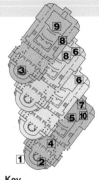

Key
▨	First Floor
▨	Second Floor
▨	Third Floor
▨	Fourth Floor

Theater
⑦ The theater has a magnificent stage curtain made by Tiffany & Co. of New York. The depiction of the Valley of Mexico on the curtain is formed with a million pieces of opalescent glass. The stunning crystal ceiling depicts Apollo and the nine muses on Mount Olympus.

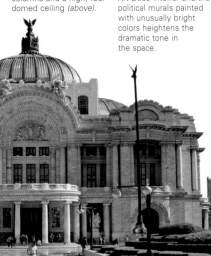

Museo Nacional de Arquitectura
⑨ This museum occupies the fourth floor of the *palacio*. Changing exhibits feature various aspects of Mexico City, and occasionally, international architecture.

Ballet Folklórico de México
⑩ Folk dances from many regions of Mexico are presented on Wednesday and Sunday evenings by the excellent Ballet Folklórico. Colorful costumes, lively music, choreography, and stage sets offer fine entertainment.

Art Exhibitions
⑧ The second and third floors have several rooms and galleries that host international travelling art exhibitions. One exceptional exhibition featured four centuries of European masterpieces in oil (below).

Mural Controversy
Diego Rivera, an avowed communist, was commissioned to paint a mural for the Rockefeller Center, New York. Nelson Rockefeller, a staunch capitalist, approved Rivera's preliminary drawings but when Rivera later included a portrait of Lenin in the mural, Rockefeller insisted that Lenin be removed. Rivera refused, and the mural was destroyed. Rivera reproduced the mural on the third floor of the *palacio* with the title *Man, Controller of the Universe*.

Construction of the Palacio de Bellas Artes began in 1904, was interrupted by the Mexican Revolution, and completed in 1934

🔟 Bosque de Chapultepec

Since the arrival of the Aztecs, Chapultepec has been a special place for residents. Today this 1,600-acre (648-hectare) green urban park includes woodlands, forest, lakes, gardens, and walking paths, and provides an abundance of activities for the entire family. Los Pinos, at the edge of the park, is the official residence of Mexico's President.

Paddle Boats, Lago de Chapultepec

🌀 Sunday is the busiest day in the park.

The Turibus route winds through the park with stops near the major attractions.

🍽 Dine with a view of the lake at Meridiem on Lago Mayor *(see p87)*, or enjoy the café at the Museo Nacional de Antropología.

• Map D4
• Main entrance at the west end of Paseo de la Reforma
• Museo Tecnológico de la CFE: Map C5; Section 2, Bosque de Chapultepec; 5516-0965; 9am–4:15pm daily; Free
• La Feria de Chapultepec: Map C5; Section 2, Bosque de Chapultepec; 5230-2121; 10am–6pm Tue–Sun (7pm Sat, 8pm Sun); Adm
• Museo de Historia Natural: Map B6; Section 2, Bosque de Chapultepec; 5515-2222; 10am–5pm Tue–Sun; Adm, free Tue
• www.chapultepec.com.mx

Top 10 Features

1. Museo Nacional de Antropología
2. Castillo de Chapultepec
3. Hot-Air Balloon Rides
4. Zoológico de Chapultepec
5. Monumento a Los Niños Héroes
6. Papalote Museo del Niño
7. Museo Tecnológico de la CFE
8. Lago de Chapultepec, Lago Mayor, and Lago Menor
9. La Feria de Chapultepec
10. Museo de Historia Natural

Museo Nacional de Antropología

Mexico's largest museum, this archeological treasure trove has 12 halls filled with brilliant artifacts that relate each significant chapter in Mexico's pre-Hispanic human history *(see pp8–9)*.

Castillo de Chapultepec

The former residence of Mexican presidents, the stunning castle *(see pp24–5)* with sweeping terraces and manicured gardens, now houses the Museo Nacional de Historia.

Hot-Air Balloon Rides

This tethered balloon rises 400 ft (123 m), offering awesome views of the park and Mexico City. On a clear day, it is the ideal place to take panoramic shots of the city.

Zoológico de Chapultepec

This excellent zoo houses more than 2,000 animals in natural habitats, and is renowned for its successful captive breeding of giant pandas. Broad shady paths, excellent viewing areas, and food courts make this a nice place to spend a few hours. Rare animals like Mexican naked dogs and native wolves can be seen here *(see p84)*.

 Chapultepec means grasshopper hill in Náhuatl, the language of the Aztecs

5 Monumento a Los Niños Héroes

On the eastern entrance to the park six pillars topped with black eagles commemorate the heroic deaths of six young cadets during the US invasion of Mexico *(see p84)*.

8 Lago de Chapultepec, Lago Mayor, and Lago Menor

The lakes are one of the most popular features of the park, and on weekends they take on a festive air. Hundreds of couples and families walk the shady paths surrounding them or take to the water in colorful rental kayaks, rowboats, and paddleboats. The walkways are filled with vendors selling their wares.

6 Papalote Museo del Niño

One of the best children's museums, this colorful and engaging museum has over 250 interactive exhibits based on the themes of science, technology, and art. New attractions are added every year. There is also an IMAX Theater with ten shows daily *(see p85)*.

7 Museo Tecnológico de la CFE

This museum highlights the developments in Mexican industry, science, and technology. A detailed scale model of an electricity generating plant, railway exhibits with train cars and engines, and oil drilling equipment are the major draws of the museum.

9 La Feria de Chapultepec

More than 50 thrilling games and rides including bumper cars, a haunted house, and a traditional roller coaster can be enjoyed at this amusement park.

10 Museo de Historia Natural

Several huge pastel colored domes *(above)* contain a wealth of exhibits covering the natural world from the creation of the universe to the evolution of life and the world around us.

Los Pinos

The official residence of the President of Mexico was moved from the Castillo de Chapultepec to Los Pinos in 1935 by President Lázaro Cárdenas, when he decided to turn the Castillo into a museum for the public. The museum has two sections – the Alcázar and the Castillo. President Cárdenas selected an existing estate within Bosque de Chapultepec, La Hormiga, as the official presidential residence. He planted numerous pine trees on the estate, and changed the name to Los Pinos. Today this lovely estate is heavily guarded and not open to the public.

Left **Gardens and fountains** Center **Garden of the Keep** Right *La Batalla de Zacatecas*, A. Bolivar

🔟 Castillo de Chapultepec

1 Museo Nacional de Historia – Alcázar Section

The lavish east wing of the Castillo, known as the Alcázar, was the Presidential Residence and Mansion of Mexican leaders from 1864 through 1939. The Alcázar and its gardens have been preserved to illustrate the lifestyle of the early presidents. The personal articles of former Mexican presidents are displayed in 23 opulent rooms *(see p83)*.

2 Museo Nacional de Historia – Castillo Section

This section of the museum is based on the oldest portion of the Castillo. The first floor's rooms present Mexico's turbulent history from the Spanish conquest through the Revolution. The second floor has two rooms featuring cultural and social displays from 1759–1917 *(see p83)*.

3 Museo del Caracol

The Galería de Historia is known as Museo del Caracol because the building is shaped like a snail. A spiral walkway is lined with exhibits that portray the struggle for Mexican independence through the Revolution up to the mid-20th century. ◉ *Section 1, Bosque de Chapultepec • Map E4 • 4040-5241 • 9am–4:15pm Tue–Sun • Adm, free Sun for Mexican residents, free for seniors (over 60), children (under 13), and teachers • www.chapultepec.com.mx*

4 Staircase of the Lions

This elegant staircase with marble lions at the base provides access to the rooftop Garden of the Keep. The staircase was built in 1878 to provide access to the National Observatory, and was remodeled in 1906 when the lions and statuary were added.

Staircase of the Lions, Alcázar Section

5 Stained-Glass Windows

The east wing has five exquisite French stained-glass windows. The windows at the top of the Staircase of the Lions have Mexican crests, one of an eagle perched on a cactus devouring a snake, and two with a grasshopper, denoting Chapultepec (Grasshopper) Hill.

Stained-glass window

6 West Terrace

The terrace on the Castillo's west side is landscaped with a lovely flower garden filled with fountains and statues. The front balcony offers wonderful views of Lago de Chapultepec and vistas out across the park.

Main Staircase

A dramatic double staircase with stone steps and wood-capped brass railings leads to the museum's Castillo Section. The upper level is decorated with stunning stained-glass windows and colorful murals.

Mural of the Niños Héroes on main staircase

Tall Knight and Garden of the Keep

This lovely formal garden offers views out over the city. The Tall Knight, in the center of the garden, was added in 1876.

South Terrace

This broad terrace is best known for the Monumento a los Niños Héroes which was added in the 1930s. The Fountain of the Grasshopper is located right in the center of this grand, sprawling terrace.

Casa de los Espejos

A handsome building, this is also known as the House of Mirrors after the 16 concave and convex mirrors inside. They distort the features of those who look into them. ◉ *At the bottom of the road leading to the Castillo*

Top 10 Alcázar Rooms

1. Dining Room with china from Díaz era
2. Ambassadors' Reception Hall with French furniture
3. Reading Room with Emperor Maximilian I's monogrammed books
4. Game Room collection gifted to Maximilian I
5. Smoking Room decorated in 19th-century style
6. Carlota's Bedchamber with Maximilian I's magnificent brass bed
7. Council Room and the office used by various former presidents
8. Díaz's Bedchamber decorated in French Empire style
9. Carmen's Bedchamber used by Díaz's wife
10. The President's Office used by Díaz

Alcázar

Viceroy Bernardo de Gálvez had the first castle built on Chapultepec Hill in 1785, but the building remained unfinished. In 1841 construction resumed, creating a Military Academy. Emperor Maximilian I came into power in 1864 and refurbished the Castillo as his personal residence, creating a luxurious European-style castle with terraced gardens and patios. Expensive furnishings were ordered from Paris, Vienna, and Italy. Later Porfirio Díaz remodeled and extended the castle. The castle continued to be used as a Presidential Mansion until 1939, when President Lázaro Cárdenas moved to a smaller residence and proclaimed the castle as the headquarters of the National History Museum. In 1940 the eastern section, the Alcázar, became a museum illustrating the lifestyle of the former presidents.

Artwork on the wall of a patio, Alcázar

An upper room of the Museo Nacional de Historia displays a collection of objects acquired from Tsar Nicholas by Porfirio Díaz

⭐10 Museo Nacional de Arte

Presenting the most important Mexican art collection in the world, the Museo Nacional de Arte is housed in a majestic Renaissance-style palacio. The collection includes the Paintings of New Spain (1550–1810), the art of the 19th century – Building the Nation (1810–1900) – and Modern Mexico (1900–1954).

A gallery in the Museo Nacional de Arte

⚙ On the top floor to the right of the staircase there is a small orientation room, where you can see the artistic evolution of the famous statues by Tolsá and Sebastián, both known as *El Caballito* (The Little Horse).

🍴 There are many restaurants nearby. Try El Cardenal, Hostería de Santo Domingo, or Café Tacuba for traditional Mexican food, or Sanborns for a quick Mexican meal *(for all, see p73)*.

- Map P2
- Tacuba 8, Col Centro
- 5130-3400
- Metro 2, 8 Bellas Artes; Turibus Plaza Manuel Tolsa-Munal #10
- 10:30am–5:30pm Tue–Sun
- 33 pesos (half-price for students and teachers), free Sun
- www.munal.com.mx

Top 10 Features

1. Palacio de Comunicaciones
2. The Virgin of the Apocalypse (1760)
3. El Caballito (1803)
4. The Torture of Cuauhtémoc (1893)
5. The Valley of Mexico from the Santa Isabel Mountain Range (1875)
6. Malgré Tout (1898)
7. Apotheosis of Peace (1903)
8. The Offering (1913)
9. The Cloud (1931)
10. The Hot-Air Balloon (1930)

Palacio de Comunicaciones

Built in an eclectic style the interior of this imposing *palacio* has a soaring staircase decorated with intricate wrought iron work. Glorious paintings adorn the building's ceilings.

The Virgin of the Apocalypse (1760)

Painted at the height of his career, Miguel Cabrera used intense color to portray the theme of *The Virgin of the Apocalypse* triumphing over evil *(below)*.

El Caballito (1803)

El Caballito or "The Little Horse," *(above)* Manuel Tolsá's famous statue, is of King Carlos IV of Spain, dressed in Roman clothing astride his horse.

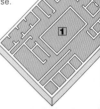

The Torture of Cuauhtémoc (1893)

Following the War of Reform in 1861 the new government placed a cultural emphasis on the history of pre-Hispanic Mexico, and by 1893 ancient Mexico was being presented as having had a glorious past. This monumental sized painting *(above)* by Leandro Izaguirre depicts the legend of Cuauhtémoc, the last Aztec Emperor, and his torture by the Spanish.

The Valley of Mexico from the Santa Isabel Mountain Range (1875)

José María Velasco painted this scene directly from nature, a first for this skilled and highly acclaimed landscape artist *(above)*.

Apotheosis of Peace (1903)

In this monumental work *(below)* Alberto Fuster celebrates the years of peace Mexico enjoyed during the reign of Díaz by comparing Mexico to ancient Greece. Neo-Classical in style, the painting mimics the opaque colors found on Renaissance frescos.

The Cloud (1931)

Gerardo Murillo, best known as Dr. ATL, is one of the most important Mexican landscape artists. He developed Altcolors, a mixture of pigment and resin that he used on many different surfaces and especially for his landscapes. *The Cloud* was painted at the height of his artistic prowess.

The Hot-Air Balloon (1930)

In bright colors and exquisite detail, this painting by Ramón Cano Manilla depicts people in traditional dress, authentic buildings and landscape, and a hot-air balloon decorated in the National colors.

Key

▨	First Floor
▨	Second Floor
▨	Third Floor

Malgré Tout (1898)

Jesús F. Contreras was one of the first Mexican sculptors to embrace modernism. He studied in France for a time, and familiarized himself with the works of Auguste Rodin. *Malgré Tout*, a magnificent marble sculpture, portrays a beautiful woman shackled and bound, still straining and yearning for freedom *(below)*.

The Offering (1913)

Saturnino Herrán turned down a scholarship for study in Europe, choosing to remain in Mexico. In this masterpiece of Modernist Nationalism, he captures the unfolding of life. An old man, a youth, and a baby are travelling through life in a Xochimilco-style barge filled with marigolds, flowers traditionally associated with death *(above)*.

Museum Guide

Enter the museum from Plaza Manuel Tolsá, pausing to look at *El Caballito* (The Little Horse), by Manuel Tolsá in the plaza, just in front of the museum. Proceed to the grand central staircase and walk up to the top floor to admire the stunning mural on the ceiling. Walk into the reception hall straight ahead to look at the ceiling mural there. Walk through the halls on this floor in sequence to get the most out of your visit. Plan to spend most of your time on the second floor where you can see the development of unique Mexican artistic styles.

Xochimilco Floating Gardens

Every weekend, visitors and the residents of Mexico City flock to Xochimilco to relax, party, and have fun. Aboard colorfully decorated trajineras (flat boats), they enjoy the beauty of these ancient canals built by the Aztecs. The floating gatherings are attended to by food and beverage vendors, musicians, and craft merchants.

Colorful *trajineras* at an *embarcadero*

Flower vendor

🌀 A pedicab is a fun way to reach the *embarcaderos* from Xochimilco village. Bus tours to the floating gardens provide an instant group of friends.

Many of the vendors and musicians wear brilliant costumes or native clothing. Photographers are expected to pay for taking their pictures.

🍴 Have a floating picnic and sample the food offered by vendors on boats.

• Map C4
• Nuevo Nativitas, Zacapa, Salitre, and Caltongo, the main embarcaderos, are near the center of Xochimilco; embarcadero Cuemanco leads to Parque Ecológico de Xochimilco
• Metro 2 to Tasqueña; then Light Rail to the outskirts of Xochimilco village; taxi or pedicab to the embarcaderos
• 200 pesos
• www.xochimilco.df. gob.mx/turismo/index. html

Top 10 Features

1. Boat Ride
2. Embarcaderos and Trajineras
3. Floating Mariachis
4. Shrines
5. Floating Food Vendors
6. Flowers for Women
7. Floating Crafts Vendors
8. Flower Gardens and Nurseries
9. Parque Ecológico de Xochimilco
10. Waterside Markets and Restaurants

Boat Ride

A boat trip through the canals in a colorful *trajinera* is the best way to experience the floating gardens of Xochimilco. Explore the festive commercial area as well as the quieter places farther from the landing.

Embarcaderos and Trajineras

The flat-bottomed boats are painted with colorful flower motifs. Several *embarcaderos* (boat jetties) are found near the center of town. Nativitas is the largest and busiest.

Floating Mariachis

Mariachi groups and *marimba* bands travel up and down the canals. On being hired, the leader boards your boat to dance and sing, accompanied by a boatload of musicians tied alongside.

Shrines
At the *embarcaderos* and along some canals can be found small, well-decorated shrines filled with flowers honoring the boaters' patron saints.

Floating Crafts Vendors
Brilliant rugs, colorful ceramics, and all manner of hand-crafted items and jewelry are also available for sale on small boats. Vendors float by, holding their wares up for all to see, and will come alongside, when invited, to give you a closer look at the selection on offer.

Parque Ecológico de Xochimilco
For a different experience, head to *embarcadero* Cuemanco where you can float in relative peace and quiet through protected areas of pristine natural beauty. It is also popular with birdwatchers.

Waterside Markets and Restaurants
The *embarcadero* Nativitas has a bustling shore-side market selling souvenirs and some good restaurants that can be easily reached by boat.

Floating Food Vendors
Vendors in small boats offer food for your table. Many have kitchens onboard with hot soup pots or grills to serve freshly cooked favorites. Other boats supply beer and soft drinks.

Flower Gardens and Nurseries
Flower gardens, greenhouses, and nurseries are found all along the banks of the canals. The flowers grown here are shipped to Mexico City and throughout the Americas.

Flowers for Women
It is traditional to give flowers to the women in your party, and flower sellers float past offering a selection of colorful blooms.

Chinampas
The Xochimilcas devised a unique method of farming. They built rafts with tree limbs and reeds, piled rich lake mud onto the rafts and then planted fast-growing trees with a deep root system in the soil. As the trees grew, the rafts became anchored to the lake bed. These *chinampas*, or floating gardens, were soon thriving, growing crops and flowers. After the Spanish conquest, Xochimilco was spared destruction because it was the main source of the city's food.

Widened for the 1968 Olympics, the canals near Cuemanco are favored by kayakers and rowing teams

10 Villa de Guadalupe

The holiest Roman Catholic shrine in Latin America is also the most visited in the world. It was here in 1531 that an Aztec peasant named Juan Diego claimed to have seen a vision of the beautiful Virgin who requested that a chapel be built. Over the centuries, pilgrims and the faithful have come to worship the Virgin of Guadalupe.

Carillón, the stone cross, Villa de Guadalupe

🕒 **Día de Nuestra Señora de Guadalupe (Dec 12)** is a national holiday and the busiest day of the year with thousands of pilgrims making the trip to Villa de Guadalupe. December is also the busiest month.

The shop in the Nueva Basílica sells an excellent selection of religious objects, books, and prints.

🍴 Food is available from many street vendors in the area, but a better bet is to eat before or after your visit.

- Map C2
- Plaza de las Américas 1
- 5577-6022
- Metro 6 La Villa-Basílica
- 6am–9pm daily
- Free; Museum 5 pesos (free for children under 12)
- www.virgende guadalupe.org.mx; www.mubagua.org.mx

Top 10 Features

1. Nueva Basílica
2. Nuestra Señora de Guadalupe
3. Antigua Basílica
4. Parroquia de Capuchinas
5. Museo de la Basílica de Guadalupe
6. Parroquia de Indios
7. Capilla del Pocito
8. Tepeyac
9. Garden and Walkway
10. Carillón

Interior, Iglesia del Cerrito, Tepeyac (Little Hill)

Nueva Basílica
This basilica was consecrated in 1976. The ground here is very soft, and the circular design, symbolizing the universality of God, also helps in evenly distributing the weight of the church *(below)*.

Nuestra Señora de Guadalupe
The original image of the Virgin on the cloak of Juan Diego *(right)* is mounted high on the wall behind the main altar. Viewers stand on moving walkways that pass below the image.

Antigua Basílica
This Baroque temple with four towers and a central tiled dome was consecrated in 1709. Designed by Pedro de Arríeta, the four domed-towers and other design elements are similar to those found in the temple of Solomon in Jerusalem. In 1904 it became a basilica in recognition of the devotion of the faithful.

It was reopened in 2000 after being closed for many years while structural supports were added to protect it from the ever increasing tilt as it sank into the soft soil.

⮕ *Pedro Ramírez Vázquez, the famous Mexican architect, designed the Nueva Basílica*

Parroquia de Capuchinas

Initially a convent for Capuchin nuns and then used as a hospital, it became a parish church in 1929 *(above)*.

Museo de la Basílica de Guadalupe

The collections in this interesting museum are primarily of artistic religious objects related to Our Lady of Guadalupe. There are paintings, sculptures, textiles, and carvings. There is also a collection of paintings by artists including Cabrera, Villalpando, and Correa.

Parroquia de Indios

This chapel dates from 1649 and in the small sacristy on the right can be seen the remains of the foundations of the original chapel built in 1531. Juan Diego lived his final years in this place, and the chapel is frequently referred to as the Chapel of Juan Diego *(below)*.

Capilla del Pocito

Our Lady of Guadalupe appeared to Juan Diego at the spring housed in this lovely circular chapel. Built in 1791, the dome is decorated with blue and white tiles.

Garden and Walkway

A tiled walkway with stairs and ramps was built to direct the flow of people to the Little Hill. Near the base of the staircase leading up the hill is a lovely rose garden. The path returning from The Little Hill curves through a large garden area with fountains and statues *(below)*.

Tepeyac

Juan Diego found the roses which appeared miraculously in winter on the top of Tepeyac, the Little Hill. Capilla del Cerrito was built in 1749 on the site. Fernando Leal painted seven murals depicting the story of the appearance of the Virgin to Juan Diego.

Carrillón

The huge stone cross at the far end of the plaza has bells that ring every hour, and has four different ways of telling time. There is a modern clock, an astronomical clock, a sun dial, and an Aztec calendar clock with 18 months of 20 days.

> ### Juan Diego's Vision
>
> When Juan Diego told the local bishop about the story of the vision, he was met with skepticism. The Virgin reappeared to Diego and told him to gather flowers, and although it was winter, Spanish roses were blooming at Tepeyac. When Diego opened his cloak to show the bishop the unseasonal flowers, an image of the Virgin was miraculously imprinted on his cloak. The prelate was convinced.

Juan Diego was canonized in 2002, becoming the first indigenous saint in the Americas

_{TOP}10 Teotihuacán

Founded around 100 BC, Teotihuacán became Mesoamerica's cultural and commercial center. At its peak – around AD 650 – it covered 8 sq miles (20 sq km) and included pyramids, temples, and housing for 200,000 people. However, very little is known about this great civilization and why they eventually abandoned the city.

Partially restored mural depicting feathered coyotes

Jaguar Mural, along the Avenue of the Dead

🗺 Many Mexico City travel agencies offer sightseeing bus tours to Teotihuacán daily.

The best view of the ruins is from the top of the Pyramid of the Moon.

There is a tram that stops at the major attractions.

🍴 There is a restaurant and café at the Visitor Center.

• Mexico State: Las Pirámides, Mex 132D (toll), 29 miles (47 km) NE of Mexico City
• (594) 956-0052
• Metro 5 to Autobuses del Norte. Then take Bus marked "Pirámides" from Central de Autobuses del Norte in Mexico City
• 8am–4:30pm daily
• 51 pesos
• Museum 8am–5pm daily, tram 30 pesos
• www.visitmexico.com

Top 10 Features

1 Pyramid of the Sun
2 Pyramid of the Moon
3 Avenue of the Dead
4 Quetzalpapalotl Palace Complex
5 Temple of Quetzalcoatl
6 Museum
7 Ciudadela
8 Palace of Temantitla
9 Tetitla
10 Atetelco

Pyramid of the Sun

The pyramid's base measures 738 ft (225 m) along each side. A tunnel under the main staircase leads to small chambers of ceremonial importance. A monumental staircase with 248 steep steps and five landings rises 213 ft (65 m) to a flat platform that once supported a temple.

Pyramid of the Moon

The oldest and most important pyramid stands at the north end of the Avenue of the Dead *(above)*. Archeological excavations have revealed several burial sites within, that have sacrificial victims and exquisite offerings.

Avenue of the Dead

From the Pyramid of the Moon a 1-mile (2-km) long road leads to the Citadel, and continues another 2 miles (3 km) beyond the excavations. The 131-ft (40-m) wide road is lined with nearly identical buildings which the Aztecs mistakenly believed to be tombs when they named the road. Archeologists believe that these were used to house civic, government, and religious functions *(below)*.

Teotihuacán or "Place of the Gods" was named by the Aztecs

Quetzalpapalotl Palace Complex

Three main palaces in the complex are believed to have been the residence of the Pyramid of the Moon's High Priest *(see p34)*.

Museum

The museum displays artifacts found on-site, as well as archeology, architecture, and history exhibits *(right)*. The glass floor in the main room covers a scale model of the site. Outside, the shady botanical garden is an excellent place to relax.

Tetitla

Located west of the loop road, this complex of dwellings illustrates how buildings were constructed and reconstructed over hundreds of years. Fragments of intricate murals adorn many of the walls within this compound.

Atetelco

This major dwelling complex has its own small altar, and many finely detailed murals depicting jaguars, coyotes, birds, and human figures. The complex is located to the west across the loop road.

Temple of Quetzalcoatl

The pyramid built around AD 200 is ornately decorated with sculptures of feathered serpents *(below)*, the rain god Tláloc, and the mythical crocodile-like symbols for fertile land. Numerous grave sites containing sacrificial victims and soldiers have been found within the pyramid.

Ciudadela

This huge compound with its massive central pyramid is surrounded by walls that measure 1,312 ft (400 m) on each side. The massive walls of the compound are 23-ft (7-m) high with pyramidal structures on top.

Palace of Temantitla

The most important and colorful murals of the site cover the walls of this dwelling complex. Richly detailed red, green, and yellow murals depict Tláloc and his watery universe. Other murals include a priest sowing seeds and people swimming and playing.

Site Guide

You can park in any of the five parking lots. Lot #1 is the closest to the Visitor Center. Across the road is the Citadel and Temple of Quetzalcoatl. Head north along the Avenue of the Dead, and turn to the right to visit the museum. Next proceed to the Pyramid of the Sun. Continue down the Avenue of the Dead to see the Jaguar Mural on the right side of the road and then the Pyramid of the Moon at the north end of the Avenue. Finally, explore the structures of the nearby Quetzalpapalotl Palace and complex.

Visit the Museo Nacional de Antropología to see more of the objects found at Teotihuacán **see pp8–9**

Left **Mural, Jaguar Palace** Center **Palace of Quetzalpapalotl** Right **Mural of a parrot-like bird**

TOP 10 Quetzalpapalotl Palace Complex

1 Plaza of the Moon
One of the sacred ceremonial areas in the city, the plaza lies between the Pyramid of the Moon and the Avenue of the Dead. The entrance to the Quetzalpapalotl Palace Complex is reached from the southwest corner of the plaza.

2 Entrance to the Palace of Quetzalpapalotl
A wide stone staircase leads from the Plaza of the Moon up to the covered east portico supported by large columns. The portico opens into a great antechamber that leads into the main palace complex.

3 Stone Serpent's Head
Near the top of the broad stone staircase leading to the portico, a huge carved stone serpent's head emerges from the wall in a position of prominence.

Stone serpent's head

4 Palace of Quetzalpapalotl
The largest and most elegant structure in the palace complex, this is believed to have been the high priest's residence. The original roof burned in the fires that swept the city in about AD 750.

5 Patio of the Pillars
The Palace of Quetzalpapalotl is named after the carved bird-butterfly figures that adorn the pillars of the inner portico.

6 Decorative Merlons
The top inner rim of the portico in the Patio of Pillars features numerous ornately carved stone merlons (battlements) decorated with bas-relief symbols of the calendar.

7 Temple of the Feathered Conches
This temple, located on a level below the palace, features an ornately carved stone façade and pillars decorated with bands of feathered conches and borders of four-petal flower motifs.

8 Mural of Parrot-like Bird
On the staircase leading to the three-sided courtyard in front of the Temple of the Feathered Conches is a brilliantly colored mural of a parrot-like bird watering a flower with its beak.

9 Jaguar Palace
The palace consists of a large open plaza in front of the middle temple. The nearby staircases have ramps shaped like snakes, while the sloping walls have murals of jaguars in various poses.

10 Jaguar Murals
Murals of jaguars, blowing feathered conch shells and with seashells on their flanks, adorn the sloping walls of a few rooms in the palace. In other murals, jaguars are seen lying in nets in a woman's arms.

Top 10 Stages of Development

1. **200–150 BC:** Small scattered agricultural settlements
2. **150–0 BC:** Construction of the Ceremonial Center, Sun Pyramid, and Moon Pyramid begins
3. **AD 0–150:** Completion of Sun and Moon Pyramids
4. **AD 150–200:** Planned city developed on a geometric grid; new buildings attached to Sun and Moon Pyramids
5. **AD 200–450:** Consolidation of state; government establishes control over economic, political, and religious systems
6. **AD 450–650:** Flourishing economy, expansion of buildings, murals painted, and external expansion of the state
7. **AD 650–750:** Population growth and limited agricultural land pose serious internal crises; colonization and demand for tribute emerge as external threats
8. **AD 750–800:** Decline of the power structure and migration of the officials; the city is damaged by a huge fire
9. **AD 800–950:** Population greatly diminished; city is in ruins and mostly abandoned
10. **After AD 950:** Toltec and later Aztec groups hold the ruins as sacred and use for their own religious ceremonies

History of Teotihuacán

Mystery surrounds the origins and language of the people who built the magnificent city of Teotihuacán, and how this great city came to be abandoned. Archeological discoveries show that an influx of people from other regions that occurred in 200 BC resulted in a reorganization of the agri-

Bones found in the site

cultural groups inhabiting the valley and development of the new planned city. The Ceremonial Center contains the oldest buildings, with the Pyramid of the Moon being built first, and the Temple of Quetzalcoatl the last. The city was laid out on a grid pattern, with the Avenue of the Dead running north and south, and an east-west road bisecting the city. All of the buildings were constructed in the Talud-Tablero style, and sophisticated drainage and sewage systems were built. Religion was very important, and some of the gods honored were Tláloc, god of Rain, Chalchiuhtlicue, goddess of Water, and Quetzalcoatl, the Feathered Serpent. Home to many skilled artisans and tradesmen, Teotihuacán developed trade throughout Mesoamerica, as its government also extended their rule over neighboring areas. Drought, over-population, disease, and social unrest have all been suggested as causes of the city's decline, which started about AD 650. An extensive fire around AD 750 engulfed much of the city. The buildings were never rebuilt and gradually the city was abandoned.

Detail of a wall in the Quetzalpapalotl Palace Complex

Left **The Aztec legend** Center **Moctezuma II meets Cortés** Right **Pancho Villa**

Moments in History

Early Inhabitants

A fertile volcanic valley with abundant resources, a long growing season, and pleasant climate gave rise to the sophisticated culture that built Teotihuacán *(see pp32–3)*, once the largest metropolis in the Western Hemisphere. Teotihuacán was a planned city with straight roads, plazas, government buildings, and spectacular ceremonial pyramids. The city reached the height of its powers in AD 550, but was abandoned in around AD 750.

Aztec Empire

The Aztecs arrived from the north, initially as mercenaries and workers. Around 1325 their god Huitzilopochtli advised them to settle where they found an eagle on a cactus devouring a snake. This they observed in Tenochtitlán. The Aztecs were ruthless fighters and by the 1420s controlled the beautiful and extensive city. They developed a firm hierarchy with an emperor, and their conquests spread to the east and south.

Spanish Conquest

Hernán Cortés, the Spanish conquistador, landed with his troops near Veracruz in 1519. As he marched toward Tenochtitlán, then ruled by Moctezuma II, he joined forces with the Tlaxcalans, a strong tribe that resisted Aztec dominance. After a bloody and destructive siege in 1521, Cortés was able to defeat the Aztecs.

Colonial Capital

The Spanish built Mexico City on top of the ruins of Tenochtitlán. Silver mined all over Mexico fueled the city's expansion and the building of large palaces. When the silver industry declined, the city stagnated for much of the 17th and early 18th century.

Mexican Independence

On September 16, 1810, Padre Miguel Hidalgo famously called for independence from Spain. But the city remained a royalist holdout until 1824 when a federal republic, the United States of Mexico, was formed. Turbulent years followed and from 1833 to 1855 Santa Anna became president 11 times.

Priest and revolutionist crowning Mexico

US Invasion

The USA invaded Mexico in 1847 and occupied Mexico City for ten months. During the battles in Bosque de Chapultepec *(see pp22–3)*, six young cadets, the *Niños Héroes*, leapt to their death rather than be captured.

Preceding pages **Pyramid of the Sun, Teotihuacán**

The Storming of Chapultepec, 1847

7 War of Reform

Mexico's most loved leader, Benito Juárez, came to power in 1855. He enacted laws that restricted the power of the Church. A bitter war ensued, and finally in 1861 the liberals won and Juárez was elected President.

8 The Maximillian Affair

In 1863, a French army invaded Mexico and the brief rule of Austrian Emperor Maximilian I began before he was deposed and executed in 1867. In those four years he remodelled the Castillo de Chapultepec (see pp24–5) and built the boulevard, today called Paseo de la Reforma (see pp74–7). After the Republic was restored, Juárez returned to power until his death in 1872.

9 Mexican Revolution

Dictator Porfirio Díaz came to power in 1872. Authoritarian yet visionary, he modernized the education and transportation systems. But the divide between rich and poor increased, and when the Díaz government annulled the 1910 victory by opponent Francisco I. Madero, the Mexican Revolution began.

10 Twentieth Century Growth and Reform

The Revolution ended with Álvaro Obregón taking control in 1920. Under the ensuing stable government, Mexico flourished and its capital grew exponentially, and it continues to grow today.

Top 10 Historical Figures

1 Emperor Moctezuma II (1466–1520)
Expanded the Aztec empire. The Spanish captured him in a battle and later killed him.

2 Hernán Cortés (1485–1547)
His successful invasion of Mexico began the Spanish colonization of the Americas.

3 La Malinche (1496–1529)
The indigenous woman who accompanied Cortés as interpreter and advisor (see p90).

4 Miguel Hidalgo y Costilla (1753–1811)
A priest, he is famous for his call to arms for independence.

5 Santa Anna (1794–1876)
Mexican military leader and 11 time president – the last in 1853.

6 Benito Juárez (1806–72)
The most loved president, he restored the republic and modernized Mexico.

7 Emperor Maximilian I (1832–67)
From Austria's imperial family, he briefly became Emperor in 1864 before being executed.

8 Porfirio Díaz (1830–1915)
Army general and president, he initiated many reforms and modernized Mexico.

9 Pancho Villa (1878–1923)
Mexican folk hero, he was one of the foremost leaders of the Mexican Revolution.

10 Francisco I. Madero (1873–1913)
A politician, he opposed the rule of Porfirio Díaz but was soon deposed and executed.

Mexico City's Top 10

Many public buildings of Centro Histórico were Church properties re-purposed or rebuilt after the War of Reforms (1857–61)

Left **Courtyard, Antiguo Colegio de San Ildefonso** Right **Gardens, Castillo de Chapultepec**

📖 Historic Sites

1 Iglesia y Hospital de Jesús Nazareno
The tomb of Hernán Cortés lies here. To the rear of the church is the place where Moctezuma II met Cortés in 1519. Half a block south is the Hospital de Jesús Nazareno, built on Cortés' command in 1524 to treat Spanish soldiers. ✆ 20 de Noviembre 82 • Map Q4 • 9am–6pm Mon–Sat • Free

Casa de la Primera Imprenta de América

2 Castillo de Chapultepec
In 1841 the building was repaired and adapted for use as a military academy. The last battle of the US invasion of Mexico in 1847 was fought here *(see pp24–5)*.

3 Palacio Nacional
Originally the site of Aztec Emperor Moctezuma II's palace, Cortés built his own palace there after his victory. In 1562 it became the residence of Mexico's viceroys and the headquarters for all of Spain's colonial government in Mexico *(see pp14–15)*.

4 Paseo de la Reforma
The boulevard was built in the 1860s by Emperor Maximilian I to connect Castillo de Chapultepec, his official residence, with the Palacio Nacional. First known as the Causeway of the Empress, it was inspired by the Champs-Elyseés in Paris. It was renamed after the restoration of the Republic in 1867 *(see pp74–7)*.

5 Casa de la Primera Imprenta de América
Constructed in 1524, the first printing press in the Americas was installed here in 1534 by Viceroy Antonio de Mendoza. Today, the house displays a model of the press and hosts temporary exhibits. ✆ Liceniado Verdad 10 and Moneda • Map Q2 • 5522-1535 • 10am–6pm daily • Closed Aug • Free

6 Zócalo
Also known as the Plaza de la Constitución, this is the cultural, political, and historical center of the city. It was called Zócalo after only the plinth *(zócalo)* was laid of an independence monument commissioned by President Santa Anna in 1843, but never completed *(see p67)*.

7 Parque Alameda Central
This is the city's oldest park with elegant fountains and shady paths. It was once reserved for the exclusive use of the aristocracy. That practice ended after the War of Mexican Independence in 1821 *(see p68)*.

Fountain, Parque Alameda Central

Aztec dancers, concheros, frequently perform at the Zócalo accompanied by drums

Palacio de Bellas Artes

It was conceived by Porfirio Díaz to be the cultural showpiece of his regime, and construction began in 1904. But, swampy subsoil and the onset of the Mexican Revolution stopped work. By 1916 only the grand façades were completed. Construction resumed in 1932, and the building was completed in 1934 *(see pp20–21)*.

Antiguo Colegio de San Ildefonso

Originally built by Jesuit friars in 1588, the property was seized by the Spanish in 1767. After independence it became a National Preparatory School. Elected president in 1920, the reformist Álvaro Obregón wanted art to mend the country and by 1922 muralists were hired to decorate the interior walls. Diego Rivera, David Alfaro Siqueiros, and José Clemente Orozco painted some of the best examples of Mexico's muralist movement here *(see p68)*.

Plaza Santo Domingo

Plaza Santo Domingo

One of the oldest colonial plazas, it is best known today for the Portal de los Evangelistas, where public scribes still write business and love letters for the city's poor and illiterate. In the colonial era the plaza was surrounded by the Church and Convent of Santo Domingo, the Palace of Inquisition, and Customs Tax Collectors. ◈ *Map Q2*

Top 10 Pre-Hispanic Sites

1 Teotihuacán
The site comprises 8 sq miles (20 sq km) of pyramids and temple ruins *(see pp32–3)*.

2 Tlatelolco
The most important Aztec market of Mesoamerica, now known as Plaza de las Tres Culturas *(see p95)*.

3 Templo Mayor
The largest and most important temple stood at the center of Tenochtitlán *(see pp16–17)*.

4 Zócalo
Major market area and site of festivities during the Aztec Empire *(see p67)*.

5 Pirámide de Cuicuilco
An unusual circular pyramid at Cuicuilco, the earliest known city in the Valley of Mexico. ◈ *5606-9758 • 9am–4:40pm daily • Free*

6 Xochimilco
The canals and floating gardens were created by the Xochimilcas *(see pp28–9)*.

7 Museo Nacional de Antropología
Fascinating artifacts from different pre-Hispanic cultures of Mexico are displayed here *(see pp8–9)*.

8 Chapultepec
The highest hill in the central valley, it was a Toltec settlement *(see pp82–5)*.

9 Tenayuca
Pre-Aztec pyramid with two parallel stairways leading to the temples at the top. ◈ *Map B1 • 10am–4:30pm Tue–Sun • Adm for museum*

10 Acatitlán
One of the few intact pyramid temples in Mexico. ◈ *Map B1 • 10am–4:30pm Tue–Sun • Adm for museum*

Left **Museo Nacional de Arte** Right **Hall, Museo Franz Mayer**

🔟 Museums

1 Museo Nacional de Antropología

The largest museum in Latin America presents a great display of archeological discoveries. Each of the museum's halls represents one of the country's prominent pre-Hispanic cultures, including Aztec, Toltec, Mayan, and eight others *(see pp8–9)*.

Museo Nacional de Antropología

2 Museo de Arte Moderno

Mexico's important contributions to 20th-century Modern Art are displayed here. The artists include Diego Rivera, José Clemente Orozco, David Alfaro Siqueiros, Juan O'Gorman, Rufino Tamayo, and Frida Kahlo. Don't miss the large sculptures in the exterior garden *(see p83)*.

3 Museo Dolores Olmedo

Known for its collection of 145 works by Diego Rivera that span his entire career, this stunning 17th-century hacienda is also a house-museum with notable pre-Hispanic and Mexican folk art collections. It also houses some of Frida Kahlo's work *(see p95)*.

4 Museo Franz Mayer

This museum houses an incredible collection of decorative furnishings from the 16th through the 19th century. Gleaned from around the world by Franz Mayer, the collection contains exquisite examples of furniture and textiles, silver, ceramics, art, and sculpture. Highlights include a 19th-century Mexican silk shawl and an 18th-century earthenware bowl *(see p68)*.

5 Museo Frida Kahlo

Paintings by Frida Kahlo and Diego Rivera are displayed in Frida's blue house, where she lived and painted. Frida's illustrated diary is here, as well as some early sketches, still lifes, and unfinished portraits. Rivera's landscape *La Quebrada* (1956) is also here *(see p89)*.

Museo Frida Kahlo

6 Museo Nacional de Arte

This museum houses the best collection of four centuries of Mexican art. Featured are masterpieces by the greatest of the Mexican artists including the famous muralists, landscape, and religious artists *(see pp26–7)*.

Children love the interactive Papalote Museo del Niño **see p85**

Museo Rufino Tamayo

7 A fabulous collection of modern art and sculpture by internationally recognized artists is housed in this dramatic concrete and white marble building set in the woods of Bosque de Chapultepec. The collection features works by internationally renowned artists Pablo Picasso, Mark Rothko, Joan Miro, Fernando Botero, Isamu Noguchi, and many others. The museum also plays host to world-class traveling art exhibitions several times a year *(see p83)*.

Museo Rufino Tamayo

Museo de Arte Carrillo Gil

8 The permanent collection features paintings by early 20th-century Mexican masters, with a large number of oils by José Clemente Orozco and David Alfaro Siqueiros. These works have amazing scope, including portraits, still lifes, and political subjects. Diego Rivera's cubist-style, 1916-painting, *El Arquitecto,* is here as well. The museum is respected for its exhibitions of contemporary work by international and Mexican artists *(see p91)*.

Templo Mayor

9 The centerpiece of this museum is the huge stone disk depicting the dismembered moon goddess Coyolxauhqui. The accidental discovery of this artifact triggered the massive excavation of the ruins of the Templo Mayor. Many of the offerings left in the temples for the gods are on display, including delicate ceramic objects, human skulls adorned with shell and flint, and the decorated knives of flint and obsidian that were used during human sacrifices. Antiquities collected by the Aztecs from earlier pre-Hispanic cities are also displayed *(see pp16–17)*.

Museo Nacional de Historia

10 This museum has two sections – the Alcázar and the Castillo. The vast collections of the museum are housed in the rooms of Castillo de Chapultepec, the former residence of Mexican presidents. The fascinating collections cover four centuries and are arranged chronologically. The Alcázar section is an astonishing house-museum which preserves the lavish lifestyle of Mexico's leaders from 1864 to 1939. The Castillo section offers a glimpse into the turbulent history of Mexico between the Spanish conquest under Cortés and the Mexican Revolution *(see p83)*.

Left **Palacio de Bellas Artes** Center **Antiguo Colegio de San Ildefonso** Right **BMV**

Architectural Highlights

1 Catedral Metropolitana

This magnificent cathedral reflects the changing architectural styles during its two centuries of construction. Work began in 1573, and continued until 1813. Among other styles, Baroque, Neo-Classical, and Churrigueresque are most evident *(see pp12–13)*.

Catedral Metropolitana

2 Antiguo Colegio de San Ildefonso

This imposing colonial building, with beautiful courtyards, dates from 1588. It has three stories, an impressive Baroque section with spacious patios, and a smaller part, completed in 1931, with a façade inspired by 18th-century architecture *(see p68)*.

3 Palacio de Minería

Manuel Tolsá designed this important Neo-Classical building in 1813. Highlights include the Old Chapel, Assembly Room, Dean's Gallery, Library, and the magnificent staircase. ✪ *Tacuba 5 • Map P2 • 5623-2982 • Manuel Tolsá Museum; 10am–6pm Wed–Sun • Adm • www.palaciomineria.unam.mx*

4 Palacio de Bellas Artes

Italian architect Adamo Boari planned this masterpiece of Art Nouveau construction. The exterior is a grand representation of Porfiriato architecture, named after President Porfirio Díaz who commissioned the building. The white Carrara marble building has a gleaming triple dome in bronze and an Aztec-influenced Art Deco interior resplendent with red marble *(see pp20–21)*.

5 Lotería Nacional

Innovative engineering and Art Deco design elements are highlights of this 1936 building designed by José Antonio Cuevas. It is the first building that used elastic flotation for earthquake protection. ✪ *Plaza de la Reforma 1 • Map M2 • 5140-7010 • www.loterianacional.gob.mx*

Lotería Nacional

6 Casa de los Azulejos

This 16th-century residence, in Churrigueresque style, was the Blue Palace until, in the 18th century, the exterior was covered with blue tiles. It is now called the House of Tiles. ✪ *Madero 4 • Map P2 • 5512-7824 • 7am–11pm*

Across the street from the Palacio de Minería stands Manuel Tolsá's famous sculpture, El Caballito (The Little Horse)

Museo Casa Barragán

This home and studio, designed by architect Luis Barragán in 1947, was designated a UNESCO world heritage site in 2004. The simple masonry building features an orthogonal floorplan with walls painted in bold colors. Light and shadow interplay with the colors and angles, creating dramatic patterns. ॐ *General Francisco Ramírez 14, Col Ampliación Daniel Garza • Map D6 • 5515-4908 • 10am–2pm & 4–6pm Mon–Fri, 10am–1pm Sat, by appointment only • Adm • http://casaluisbarragan.org*

Universidad Nacional Autónoma de México (UNAM)

In the late 1940s, 60 architects were enlisted to design 20 buildings and sports complexes for the new university to the south of Mexico City. The highlight is the Central Library designed by Juan O'Gorman. ॐ *Ciudad Universitaria • Map B3 • 5622-1086 • 8am–8:30pm daily • Free • Closed public holidays • http://unam.mx*

Bolsa Mexicana de Valores (BMV)

To an unfinished structure planned as a hotel, the architect Juan José Díaz added height, giving it an angled appearance. The dramatic wedge-shaped tower and spherical dome of the Mexican Stock Exchange are covered with shimmering black and dark blue mirrored glass. Trading takes place under the dome, while the offices are located in the tower. ॐ *Paseo de la Reforma 255 • Map J4 • http://bmv.com.mx*

Torre Mayor with the Diana Fountain in front

Torre Mayor

Mexico City's tallest building towers 740 ft (225 m) on the Paseo de la Reforma. The gracefully curved front façade is made with 323,000 sq ft (30,000 sq m) of glass, and supported by a traditional granite skyscraper. The design of this 55-story contemporary office building uses anti-seismic technology in order to help it withstand an earthquake of up to 8.5 on the Richter scale. ॐ *Paseo de la Reforma 505 • Map F3 • www.torremayor.com.mx*

Left **Lago Mayor, Bosque de Chapultepec** Right **Parque Alameda Central**

🔟 Parks, Gardens, and Courtyards

1 Bosque de Chapultepec

This huge and diverse urban park offers a fantastic selection of activities and makes a perfect escape from the hustle and bustle of the city. Most of the major museums and the zoo are located in the first section. Two other sections offer more green space, fewer visitors, and are ideal for walking, cycling, and boating *(see pp22–3)*.

2 Parque Alameda Central

Landscaped with poplar, ash, willow, and jacaranda trees, this lovely green park is a shady oasis adorned with fountains, sculptures, and paved walkways that attract both locals and tourists *(see p68)*.

Obregón Memorial, Jardín de la Bombilla

3 Parque México

This park is a great place for joggers and walkers who want to avoid the crowds. Built on the site of a former horse racetrack, the large park has attractive landscaping and shady paths. 🆂 *Av México and Av Sonora, Col Condesa • Map H5*

4 Parque Ecológico de Xochimilco

This less-commercialized zone of Xochimilco provides a view of the ancient system of water canals and man-made islands developed by the Aztecs. Flower gardens and a bird preserve are added attractions *(see p28–9)*.

5 Jardín de la Tercera Edad and Jardín Botánico

Set aside for senior citizens, Jardín de la Tercera Edad is the oldest botanical garden within Bosque de Chapultepec. There is a walking path lined with 36 sculptures, an orchid pavilion, and a greenhouse. There is also a public garden, Jardín Botánico, with a lush tropical conservatory. 🆂 *Paseo de la Reforma and Calzada Chivatito • Map D3, D4*

6 Jardín de la Bombilla

This peaceful San Ángel park has walking paths and benches beneath shade trees. In the center of the park there is a huge monument in memory of Álvaro Obregón, hero of the Mexican Revolution, who became President in 1920. 🆂 *Av Insurgentes Sur and Arenal • Map T3*

Parque México

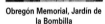 Hire a boat or bicycle to explore the canals and walking paths of the Parque Ecológico de Xochimilco

Jardín del Centenario

7 The atrium of the former convent of the church of San Juan Bautista is today a lovely town park in Coyoacán. In the center of the park stands the Fountain of Coyoacán with sculptures of two coyotes. ◈ *Centenario and Felipe Carillo Puerto • Map W2*

Archway, Jardín del Centenario

Viveros de Coyoacán

8 Once the private nurseries of environmentalist Miguel Ángel de Quevedo, today it raises seedling trees for the entire city. Joggers and walkers enjoy the mile-long dirt path that curves through the park. It is also popular with bird-watchers. ◈ *Map V2 • 8am–5pm daily*

Parque Hundido

9 A favorite with walkers and joggers, the park was formerly a clay-quarry. More than 50 replicas of pre-Columbian sculpture were placed along the pathways in the 1970s. ◈ *Av Insurgentes Sur and Av Porfirio Díaz • Map B3*

Jardín Botánico

10 This botanical garden, located next to the University (UNAM) Stadium, features Mexican flora and ornamental plants. The garden is organized by climate zones. The specialty gardens for medicinal and native plants are highlights here. There is also a greenhouse in the garden *(see p45).*

Top 10 Courtyards and Small Gardens

1 Plaza de la Santa Veracruz
A quiet, pleasant spot to sit and listen to the fountain. ◈ *Av Hidalgo • Map N2*

2 Museo Franz Mayer Courtyard
Surrounded by two-story porticoes it has a central, tiled stone fountain *(see p68).*

3 Jardín Botánico in Palacio Nacional
This large inner courtyard has large, beautiful gardens *(see pp14–15).*

4 Sculpture Garden
A garden plaza with ten huge bronze sculptures. ◈ *Av Francisco I. Madero*

5 Jardín de la Solidaridad
Commemorates the people who lost their lives in the devastating 1985 earthquake. ◈ *Zarco y Hidalgo*

6 Gardens of Palacio de Bellas Artes
These flower gardens are ideal to enjoy the surrounding beauty *(see pp20–21).*

7 Courtyard of San Angel Inn
Inner courtyard of the former monastery *(see p93).*

8 Courtyard of the Museo SCHP
An inner courtyard with ancient trees and stone fountains *(see p69).*

9 Parque Lincoln
This park has a botanical garden, ponds, and an art gallery. ◈ *Emilio Castelar and Luis G. Urbina*

10 Monastery Gardens at Parque Nacional Desierto de los Leones
The gardens are ideal to listen to birdsong *(see p96).*

Left **Altar, Templo de la Enseñanza** Right **Catedral Metropolitana**

TOP 10 Churches

1 Antigua Basílica de Guadalupe

This basilica honors the Virgin of Guadalupe, Mexico's patron saint. In 1531 the Virgin appeared to a native, Juan Diego, requesting a church be built there. Diego convinced the local priest by showing him a cape bearing the image of the Virgin. Antigua Basílica de Guadalupe was built in 1709. The cape is displayed in the new basilica, built in 1976 (see pp30–31).

Antigua Basílica de Guadalupe

2 Catedral Metropolitana

The largest colonial cathedral in the Americas dominates the Zócalo in the center of Mexico City. The Spanish Baroque façade, with 18 bells in its twin bell towers, only hints at the splendor inside (see pp12–13).

Templo de Santo Domingo

3 Templo de Santo Domingo

The first Dominican church in the city was built here in 1530. The current Baroque church was built in 1736 with ornately carved columns and a marble carving of Santo Domingo de Guzmán above the entrance. The main altar was created by Manuel Tolsá. A side chapel contains colorful scarves left by those who have experienced a personal miracle.
◎ República de Brasil and Belisario Domínguez • Map Q1

4 Templo de la Enseñanza

Nine fabulous ultra-Baroque altarpieces fill the interior of this small church built in the 1770s. Angels surround the *Virgin of El Pilar* in the exceptional fresco adorning the high-domed ceiling above the golden main altar featuring statues of saints. The elaborate late-Baroque façade is unusually narrow and tilts backward from uneven settling.
◎ Donceles 104 • Map Q2 • 7:30–8pm Mon–Sat, 10am–2pm Sun

5 Iglesia y Ex-Convento de San Francisco

One of the best Churrigueresque façades in the city adorns the remnants of the High Convent of Our Holy Father St. Francis of Mexico. Once the largest monastery in the city, it was largely destroyed after the Reform Laws were passed in the late 1850s (see p39). Today the lovely main church has a Neo-Classical altar, stained-glass windows, and fine wood sculptures by Miguel Ángel Soto. ◎ Madero 7 • Map P3

6 Iglesia de la Profesa (San Felipe Neri)

The Mudéjar roof above the choir stalls is the only visible remains of the original 1610 Jesuit church. The church was rebuilt in 1720 and is one of the finest examples of Mexican Baroque architecture. The Neo-Classical altarpiece was created by Manuel Tolsá. ⊗ *Madero and Isabel la Católica • Map P2*

Iglesia de la Profesa

7 Templo de Regina Coeli

This masterpiece of Churrigueresque style dates from the 17th century. Three of the five altars display paintings by famous 18th-century artists, including Villalpando and Rodríguez Juárez. The elegant main altar is dedicated to Regina Coeli (Queen of Heaven) and has a fine painting of the Virgin in the center. ⊗ *Regina and Bolívar • Map P4*

8 Parroquia de San Bernardino de Siena

Dedicated to Saint Bernardine of Siena, who is believed to have interceded with God on behalf of the indigenous Mexican people, this Xochimilco church is best known for its exceptional 16th-century altarpiece *(see p97)*.

9 Ex-Convento e Iglesia del Carmen

This Carmelite church from the early 1600s was part of the del Carmen Convent. Three exterior domes decorated with colorful tiles dominate the roofline. Built in Latin Cross form, the interior walls of this narrow church are partially tiled with frescos. The colonial-era main altar is the interior's highlight *(see p90)*.

10 Iglesia de San Francisco Javier

This exceptional Mexican Baroque church was constructed in the late 1600s. The limestone façade and single-bell tower are decorated with ornately detailed stone carvings. Inside, the golden main altar is resplendent with fine decorations. Murals by Miguel Cabrera adorn the cross vaults and the chancel *(see p62)*.

Iglesia de la Profesa was consecrated as San Felipe Neri after the Jesuits' expulsion in 1767, but the former name remains in use

Tiled frescoes by Juan O'Gorman, Central Library, Universidad Nacional Autónoma de Mexico

Murals

Antiguo Colegio de San Ildefonso

In 1922, to heal political wounds through art, young artists such as Rivera, Siqueiros, and Orozco, were hired to paint murals on the walls of the school. However, some citizens did not agree with their leftist ideals (see p68).

Mexican muralist David Alfaro Siqueiros in his studio

Polyforum Siqueiros

David Alfaro Siqueiros' huge murals cover the exterior and interior walls of this ultra-modern 12-sided cultural center. In the main hall on the fourth floor is his masterpiece, the monumental, multi-dimensional *La Marcha de la Humanidad* or *The March of Humanity* (see p98).

Castillo de Chapultepec

On the first floor is the Museo Nacional de Historia which showcases excellent murals featuring aspects of Mexican history by famous muralists. Juan O'Gorman's *Retablo de la Independencia*, José Clemente Orozco's mural of Benito Juárez, and David Alfaro Siqueiros' satiric image of Porfirio Díaz are a few of the best ones (see p43).

Casa de los Azulejos

One of José Clemente Orozco's best known murals, the 1925 *Omnisciencia*, adorns the staircase of this building, now a Sanborns restaurant. One of his earlier works, it is painted in subdued tones of gold and brown (see p44).

Secretaría de Educación Pública

Diego Rivera painted more than 100 murals on three floors of this building between 1923 and 1928. It is the best place in the city to view his murals. See *Day of the Dead* in the second patio on the first floor and his self-portrait in the stairwell leading to the fourth floor. ◈ *República de Argentina 28 • Map Q2 • 3003-1000 • 9am–6pm Mon–Fri • Free*

Universidad Nacional Autónoma de México

Excellent murals by highly respected muralists decorate the exteriors of several buildings. On the Rectory Tower is David Alfaro Siqueiros' *Alegoría de la Cultura*. The tiled frescos on four façades of the Central Library building by Juan O'Gorman depict 400 years of Mexican history. Francisco Eppens Helguera's mural on the façade of the Medicine building portrays pre-Hispanic themes. On the Olympic Stadium is a high relief mural about family, peace, and sports by Diego Rivera. ◈ *Ciudad Universitaria • Map B3 • 5622-6470 • 8am–9:30pm daily • Free*

Palacio Nacional

Covering 4,800 sq ft (450 sq m) three murals, titled *Epic of the Mexican People*, are among Diego Rivera's finest and most visited. This monumental work, spanning the walls of the central staircase of the *palacio*, portrays the history of Mexico. Additional murals fill the walls of the third floor hallway *(see pp14–15)*.

Interiors of the magnificent Palacio de Bellas Artes

Palacio de Bellas Artes

Surrounding the interior courtyard of the *palacio* are works of seven muralists. David Alfaro Siqueiros' *Nueva Democracia*, Diego Rivera's *El Hombre Contralor del Universo* and José Clemente Orozco's *Mundo Contemporáneo* are the most outstanding *(see pp20–21)*.

Museo Mural Diego Rivera

Diego Rivera's famous *Dream of a Sunday Afternoon in the Alameda Central* was moved here after the earthquake of 1985 destroyed the Hotel Del Prado, where Rivera painted the mural in 1947–8. ⊙ *Balderas y Colón • Map M2 • 5518-0183 • 10am–6pm Tue–Sun • Adm, free Sun • www.museomural diegorivera.bellasartes.gob.mx/*

Museo de Arte Moderno

Oil paintings of many well-known muralists are showcased here, including works by Rivera, Orozco, Siqueiros, Tamayo, and Juan O'Gorman *(see p83)*.

Top 10 Mural Artists

1 Diego Rivera (1886–1957)
Brilliant muralist and painter, he had Marxist ideals and was a controversial revolutionary.

2 José Clemente Orozco (1883–1949)
Best known for his bold murals portraying themes of human versus mechanical.

3 Juan O'Gorman (1905–82)
Known for his murals and architecture depicting subjects from Mexican history.

4 David Alfaro Siqueiros (1896–1974)
A political activist, he infused his colorful murals with revolutionary ideas.

5 Rufino Tamayo (1899–1991)
Fused Fauvism, Cubism, folk, and pre-Hispanic Mexican styles into his murals and oils.

6 Roberto Montenegro (1887–1968)
One of the first muralists, his works dwell on Mexico's violent past.

7 Manuel Rodríguez Lozano (1896–1971)
Dedicated to establishing a true Mexican artistic style, he later protested the monopoly held by the leading muralists.

8 Francisco Eppens Helguera (1913–90)
Painter, muralist, and sculptor, his huge outdoor murals are made of colored glass tiles.

9 Jean Charlot (1898–1979)
French born, he revived and refined the fresco technique later used by Diego Rivera.

10 González Camarena (1908–81)
He specialized in colorful scenes indigenous to Mexico.

Left **Colorful sombreros** Right **Bright and vibrant flowers for sale**

🔟 Markets

Mercado Jamaica
Beautiful and vibrantly color-ful, this is the city's wholesale flower market. Every imaginable type of seasonal flower grown in the country can be seen here in dazzling abundance. Always exces-sive, the profusion of blooms of every hue reaches amazing crescendos at major holidays and festivals. ◎ *Av Morelos and Congreso de la Unión • 8am–4pm daily*

Mercado de la Merced
With crowded narrow paths between small booths offering towering piles of brilliantly colored and artfully displayed merchandise of every kind, a visit to Mexico City's main wholesale and retail market is as much a cultural experience as it is a shopping one. ◎ *Rosario and Abraham Olvera • 6am–6pm daily*

Mercado Sonora
Known as the "Witches Market", locals come to this market to buy a broad variety of herbs, herbal remedies, folk medicine, and treatments. Everything required to cast a spell, conjure up love, restore health, or obtain wealth can be found here. ◎ *South of Mercado de la Merced, across Fray Servando Teresa de Mier • 6am–6pm daily*

Mercado de Coyoacán
This neighborhood market is friendly and attractive. Many traditional Mexican wares, such as sombreros, brilliant rugs, and whimsical *piñatas* (papier-mâché figures filled with treats) are sold. The food stalls are a big attraction. On weekends there is a craft market at the Jardín del Centenario *(see p47)*. ◎ *Coyoacán, between Xicoténcatl, Abasolo, Malintzin, and Allende • Map X1 • 10am–6pm daily*

Mercado de Coyoacán

Mercado Xochitl
Lively and colorful, this neighborhood market offers meat, poultry, sausage, spices, fruits, and flowers of exceptional quality that are grown along the Xochimilco canals. ◎ *Calles Madero, 16 de Septiembre, Guerrero and Morelos • Map B4 • Daily*

Mercado Insurgentes
This indoor market is renowned for its glittering displays of fine silver jewelry, pendants, earrings, and bracelets, which are artistically arranged and brightly illuminated. There are also silver bowls, platters, tableware, and sculptures. In some booths you can watch silversmiths at work *(see p78)*.

Crowded markets attract pickpockets – always take a little more care when visiting these areas

Mercado San Juan

An artisan's cooperative, the indoor booths of the market fill two floors offering traditional handmade goods such as finely crafted silver jewelry, painted ceramics, and woven textiles.
◈ *Ayuntamiento and Aranda • Map N3 • 9am–7pm Mon–Sat, 9am–4pm Sun*

Mercado de Artesanías de la Ciudadela

The largest gathering of souvenir and handicraft vendors in the Centro Histórico area, this semi-open market offers a variety of traditional items. ◈ *Balderas and E. Dondé • Map M3 • 9am–6pm daily*

Jardín de Arte

This weekly outdoor art market in the Plaza del Carmen has artists lining the walkways with their works. Of high quality and brilliant hues, the subjects of the paintings range from historical Mexican scenes to contemporary themes. ◈ *San Ángel, Plaza del Carmen bordered by Frontera and Amargura • 9am–7pm Sat*

Paintings on sale, Jardín de Arte

Bazar de Sábado

A very popular weekly (only on Saturdays) artisan and handicrafts market, it also has a charming courtyard and an excellent restaurant. Bazar de Sábado technically refers to the skilled craftsmen in the building, however, many of the outdoor booths have excellent wares as well *(see p90)*.

Top 10 Things to Buy

Ceramics
Mexico produces a wealth of colorful pottery and ceramics, the Talavera style being the most notable.

Woven Fabrics
Look for fine shawls from San Luis Potosí, *panchos* from Saltillo and Zacatecas, and *charro* jackets from Zacatecas and Durango.

Cigars
Most upscale hotels and cigar shops sell Cuban and Mexican cigars.

Sweets
Sweet breads are offered in dazzling arrays. Fried *churros* (doughnuts), often dipped in hot chocolate, make a great treat.

Jewelry
Silver jewelry of the best quality is readily available. A stamp of "925" indicates the highest silver content.

Antiques
Furniture, silver jewelry, ceramics, paintings, and art objects are all available in antique shops in Zona Rosa, Polanco, and San Ángel.

Leather
Decorative leather jackets, belts, boots, and gloves are popular, as are saddles and bridles.

Carvings
A popular folk art, the best woodcarvings come from Oaxaca.

Liquor and Wine
Tequila and *mezcal* are internationally renowned Mexican liquors.

Other Crafts
Exquisite embroidery work, brightly painted papier-mâché figures, and tin lanterns are also available.

Ask about the artist when buying handicrafts; not everything in the markets is made in Mexico

Left **Roadside snacks** Center **Chicken** *tostada* Right *Tamales*

Cuisine

1 Central Mexican Cuisine

With intense colors and spices, Mexican cuisine blends flavors from Aztec, Spanish, African, and European heritage. Corn is the cuisine's foundation and is ground to make flour for *tamales* and *tortillas*. Other staples include beans and chilis.

2 Antojitos

A broad category of small dishes served as appetizers or snacks, a typical *antojito* could be created atop small *tortillas* or pan fried flatbreads and might include layers of spiced bean paste, sautéed herbs or chopped vegetables, cheese, and small bits of meat. It can also include small *tacos*, *tostadas,* or soups.

Chicken *enchiladas* in *mole* sauce

3 Mole

This sauce varies widely in flavor and ingredients, but usually is made with ground chilis, herbs and spices, tomatoes, and almost always a bit of chocolate. The result is a rich and complex sauce that most often accompanies chicken, turkey, or *enchiladas*.

4 Tamales

Tamales are a staple of Mexican life and are made from corn pastry rolled around a simple filling of meat and sauce or chilis. Wrapped in a corn husk for convenience, they are cooked by steaming. Street vendors often prepare them as a morning dish for workers, but restaurants also serve them as a main dish with a spicy red or green sauce.

5 Tortillas, Tacos, Tostadas, and Enchiladas

The foundation of many Mexican dishes, *tortillas* are flat circles of corn dough that are fried and rolled around a filling of meat, sauces, spices, and vegetables. *Tacos* are folded or rolled and eaten by hand. With *tostadas*, the filling is piled on a flat *tortilla* that is fried crispy, and *enchiladas* are rolled and often baked and smothered in a green (*verde*) or red (*rojo*) sauce.

6 Fruits and Cheeses

Central Mexico's year round spring-like climate is perfect for growing a wide range of fruits, and the *mercados* present a dazzling array of fresh fruits including mangoes, papayas, bananas, apples, and pineapples. Cheese, *queso*, is another staple of Mexican cuisine and each region produces its own unique cheeses. Favorites include *oaxaca*, *chihuahua*, creamy *panela,* and smooth, yellow *manchego*.

 Chilis are a key ingredient in Mexican cooking; they are used to add flavor, color, or texture and are not necessarily spicy

7 Sopas and Pozole

Most Mexican soups, *sopas*, have a chicken or tomato base. Rich herbs and spices create flavors that are uniquely Mexican. *Tortilla* soup, *albóndigas* (meatball) soup, and Mexican lime soup, are favorites. Also popular is *pozole*, a hearty and satisfying stew made from pork and corn.

Mexican soup

8 Carnes y Aves (Meat and Poultry)

Pork is slow-roasted in layers of spices and then shredded or cubed into other dishes. Beef is marinated in delicious combinations of wine, lime juice, and spices to create tender *arrachera* steaks. Chicken, be it braised, grilled, broiled, or boiled is also very popular.

9 Mariscos

Fish is often grilled and served whole with sauces and sides. Shrimps are hugely popular, served on ice with tangy sauces or as fiery *camarones diablo* over rice. Crabs, lobster, and oysters are also popular.

10 Desserts and Sweets

In Mexico City you get the flakiest pastries and the lightest puffy sweet rolls called *pan dulce*. A typical Mexican dessert is the custard-like flan. Also popular are homemade *helados* (ice creams), *sorbetes*, and desserts with rich Mexican chocolate.

Top 10 Drinks

1 Beer
Mexico produces some of the best beers in the world. Favorites include *Corona*, *Dos Equis*, and *Negra Modelo*.

2 Tequila
Mexico's national drink is made by distilling the fermented juices of the blue agave. Fiery and potent, it can sell from $4 to $400 a bottle.

3 Pulque
This drink made from fermented cactus juices can be traced back to Aztec times.

4 Horchata
This traditional iced drink, reputed to be a cure for hangovers, is made from almonds, powdered rice, cinnamon, cane sugar, and limes.

5 Wine
Mexico produces over 40 varieties of wines, many of them award-winning.

6 Coffee
Mexican coffee is rich, smooth, and full bodied. A favorite is *café con leche*.

7 Atole
A traditional hot drink made from corn starch, cane sugar, cinnamon, and sometimes chocolate.

8 Hot Chocolate
Traditional Mexican hot chocolate is made from dark chocolate, cane sugar, milk or cream, cinnamon, and ground nuts or eggs for body.

9 Fruit Juice, Licuados
Roadside vendors offer chilled juices, fresh-squeezed from a variety of fresh fruits. When the fruits are blended with milk, honey, and yogurt, you get *licuados*.

10 Aguas Frescas
Fruit juices blended with chilled water or mineral water.

Left **El Rincón del Mariachi, Plaza Garibaldi** Right **Inside a cantina**

🔟 Entertainment and Performing Arts

1 Mexican Ballet

The acclaimed Ballet Folklórico de México presents fabulously choreographed folk dances within the Art Deco opulence of the theater at the Palacio de Bellas Artes *(see pp20–21)*. Classical and modern dance and music performances are also held at the Teatro de la Danza in Polanco *(see sidebar)*.

2 Classical Music

The National Symphony Orchestra and the National Opera perform at the Palacio de Bellas Artes. The Centro Cultural Ollin Yoliztli and Sala Nezahualcóyotl host music performances. Other musical events are held at venues throughout the city, including the Auditorio Nacional *(see sidebar)* and Estadio Azteca *(see p59)*.

3 Lucha Libre

In this enjoyable spectacle, masked combatants skilfully combine wrestling, acrobatics, and pantomime. There are two types of wrestlers – "goodies" or *técnicos* and "baddies" or *rudos (see p59)*. 🅢 *Arena Coliseo: República de Perú 77 • 5526-1687* 🅢 *Arena México: Dr. La Vista • 5325-9000 • www.arenamexico.com.mx*

4 Bars and Lounges

Cantinas start filling up in the late afternoon, usually serve food, and often close by 11pm. Bar la Ópera *(see p73)* in Centro and Cantina la Coyoacana *(see p93)* in Coyoacán are popular

cantinas. Bars and lounges are busiest from midnight on. Many of the large hotels have lounges with nightly entertainment.

A well-stocked bar

5 Dance Clubs

Salsa and cumbia keep the crowds dancing until the small hours at Mama Rumba, where they also have dance classes (Wed & Thu). Trendy El Bar Mata has two floors of dancing to the sounds of jazz, blues, and rock. 🅢 *Mama Rumba: Queretáro 230, Col Roma • 5564-6920 • 9pm–2:30am Wed–Sat • Cover charge* 🅢 *El Bar Mata: Filomeno Mata 11, Col Centro • 9:30pm–3am Thu–Sat • No cover charge*

6 Dinner Shows

An intimate basement club in the Centro Histórico, Zinco offers the best live jazz in the city. La Bodega, in a former mansion in hip Colonia Condesa, is a maze of small rooms with eclectic decor. It offers a Cuban band, performances by local singers, and good Mexican food. 🅢 *Zinco: Motolinía 20 • 5512-3369* 🅢 *La Bodega: Popocatépetl 25 • 5511-7390*

At night it is advisable to use only pre-arranged hotel or sitio taxi (see p103), or bus tours; watch against pickpockets and thieves

7 Mariachi Music

The traditional late afternoon and evening place for *mariachi* music is Plaza Garibaldi in Centro Histórico where bands roam, surrounded by bronze statues of the legendary *mariachis*. Another place to enjoy their music is Xochilmilco *(see pp28–9)*.

Mariachis, Plaza Garibaldi

8 Cinema

Cinema is extremely popular in Mexico City, and prices are reasonable. Cinemex and Cinepolis are the two largest theater chains. ⊗ *Cinemex: www. cinemex.com* ⊗ *Cinepolis: www. cinepolis.com.mx*

9 Gay and Lesbian

There is a large and active gay, and to a lesser extent lesbian, community in Mexico City. The bars and discos change frequently, so it is a good idea to check the weekly *Tiempo Libre (see p102)* or the websites below for current information. ⊗ *www.sergay.com.mx and http:// gayguide.net*

10 Family

The city's ultimate family place is Bosque de Chapultepec *(see pp22–3)*. Favorites include La Feria, Museo del Niño, and Zoológico de Chapultepec. Children will enjoy the boat rides at Xochimilco Floating Gardens *(see pp28–9)* and views of Mexico City from the top of the Torre Latinoamericana *(see p71)*.

Top 10 Music and Dance Venues

1 Centro Nacional de las Artes

Hosts a variety of shows. ⊗ *Av Río Churubusco 79, Col Tlalpan • 4155-0000 ext. 1035 • www.cenart.gob.mx*

2 Auditorio Nacional

Modern auditorium with excellent acoustics. ⊗ *Paseo de la Reforma 50, Col San Miguel Chapultepec • 9138-1350 • www.auditorio.com.mx*

3 Centro Cultural Telmex

Offers Broadway plays in Spanish. ⊗ *Av Cuauhtémoc 19, Col Juárez • 5514-1965*

4 Palacio de Bellas Artes

Premier performing and cultural center *(see pp20–21)*.

5 Sala Nezahualcóyotl

Concert hall with 2,400 seats. ⊗ *Insurgentes Sur 3000, CU, UNAM • 5622-7125 • http:// musicaunam.net*

6 Centro Cultural Ollin Yoliztli

Part of an active arts complex. ⊗ *Periférico Sur 5141, Col Isidro Fabela • 5606-3901*

7 Teatro de la Danza

Stages a variety of dance and musical shows. ⊗ *Centro Cultural del Bosque, Col Polanco • 5280-8771 extn. 556*

8 Teatro Blanquita

Hosts top Mexican artists. ⊗ *Av Lázaro Cárdenas 16, Col Centro • 5325-9000, 5237-9999*

9 Teatro de los Insurgentes

A range of plays and musicals. ⊗ *Av Insurgentes Sur 1587, Col San José Insurgentes • 5611-4253 • www.teatroinsurgentes.com.mx*

10 El Lunario

Top international artists perform here. ⊗ *Paseo de la Reforma 50, Bosque de Chapultepec • www.lunario.com.mx*

Nightlife tours are offered by many hotels and travel agencies, and often include dinner, a show, and a stop at Plaza Garibaldi

Left **Jogger, Viveros de Coyoacán** Right **Hot-Air Balloon**

Outdoor Activities and Sports

Hiking
In the mountains, southwest of Mexico City, are several parks, such as Parque Nacional Desierto de los Leones *(see p96)*, Parque Nacional los Dinamos *(see p96)*, and Parque Nacional Ajusco, that offer a variety of hiking trails.
⊗ *Parque Nacional Ajusco: Camino al Ajusco from Periférico Sur*

Mountain Biking
There are many mountain-bike trails near Mexico City. Some of the most accessible are at San Nicolás Totolapan. It offers about 93 miles (150 km) of dirt trails at altitudes between 8,900 ft (2,700 m) and 12,000 ft (3,740 m).
⊗ *Picacho-Ajusco Rd • 1675-1627 • Adm • www.parquesannicolas.com.mx • Bikes on rent are available only on weekends*

Biking trail, Parque Nacional de los Leones

Rock Climbing
Parque Nacional los Dinamos *(see p96)* offers the best rock climbing near the city with many bolted and bolt-free climbing routes along the narrow gorge of the Magdalena River. Mochilazo offers guided day trips and rock climbing courses. ⊗ *Mochilazo: 5239-5485 • www.mochilazo.com.mx*

Jogging and Walking
One of the favorite places to walk and jog is the Bosque de Chapultepec *(see pp22–3)*. Viveros de Coyoacán *(see p47)*, Parque México in Condesa *(see p46)*, and Parque Hundido *(see p47)* are also popular with joggers and walkers.

Bird Watching
One of the best places for bird watching is Xochimilco *(see pp28–9)*, both along the canals and in the Parque Ecológico de Xochimilco. The pine and oak forests at Parque Nacional Desierto de los Leones *(see p96)* yields different species, including the lovely bright Red Warbler.

Hot-Air Balloons and Hang Gliding
A hot-air balloon for a tour over the Valley of Mexico or the pyramids of Teotihuacán can be arranged. For hang gliding and paragliding head to Valle de Bravo *(see p63)*. ⊗ *Globo Aventura: 5661-8919 • www.globoaventura.com* ⊗ *Flyvolare: 5331-2460 • www.flyvolare.com.mx* ⊗ *Alas del Hombre: (726) 262-6382 • www.alas.com.mx*

Horseback Riding
Many of the National Parks in the Valley of Mexico offer horseback riding on weekends and holidays. Local horse owners offer their horses for rent, and can be found at both Parque Nacional Desierto de los Leones *(see p96)* and Parque Nacional

Ajusco. In the Valle de Bravo *(see p63)* there are outfitters with horseback trips to see monarch butterflies in winter.

Parque Nacional de los Leones

Water Sports and Boating
Acapulco offers a huge variety of year-round ocean sports and activities including deep sea fishing, boating, scuba diving, and water skiing. ✪ *Acapulco Tourist Office • (744) 484-2216 • www.visiteacapulco.com*

Golf, Tennis, and Swimming
Most golf courses are members- and guests-only clubs. A golf course that does allow visitors is Campestre Cocoyoc at Hotel Hacienda Cocoyoc. Many hotels offer tennis courts and swimming pools. ✪ *Hotel Hacienda Cocoyoc: Donato Guerra 9, Tizapán, San Ángel • 5550-2202 • www.cocoyoc.com.mx*

Volcano Mountaineering
Climbing the volcanoes near Mexico City provides strenuous, but non-technical adventures. Maps and directions for these treks are primitive, but there are guides available. Popular trips include the tough climb to the top of Iztaccíhuatl *(see p63)*. Less taxing would be climbs to the top of La Malinche near Puebla or Nevado de Toluca near Valle de Bravo.
✪ *ItalianTREK: 5669-3151 • www.italiantrek.com* ✪ *Río y Montaña: 5292-5032 • www.rioymontana.com*

Top 10 Spectator Sports

1 Bullfighting
Top matadors fight the toughest bulls. ✪ *Plaza Monumental de Toros México • 5563-3959 • Sun Nov–Feb • www.lamexico.com*

2 Fútbol (Soccer)
Mexicans' favorite spectator sport. ✪ *Estadio Azteca: Calzada de Tlalpan 34000 • 5487-3100* ✪ *Estadio Universitario: Av Insurgentes Sur*

3 NBA Basketball
Palacio de los Deportes hosts exhibition games. ✪ *Av Río Churubusco and Calle Añil*

4 Professional Baseball
The home team, Diablos Rojos, plays at Foro Sol. ✪ *Av Viaducto Río de la Piedad, Col Granjas México • 5639-8722 • www.diablos.com.mx*

5 Horse Racing
Races are held at Hipódromo de las Américas. ✪ *Av Industria Militar, Col Lomas de Sotelo • 5387-0600 • Fri–Sun • www.hipodromo.com.mx*

6 Charrerías
Horsemanship events are held at Lienzo Charro. ✪ *Av Constituyentes 500 • 5277-8706 • www.nacionaldecharros.com*

7 Rowing
The Cuemanco Channel is a popular spot. ✪ *5555-4499*

8 Boxing
Bouts are held at Salón 21. ✪ *Molière, 4 Andromaco, Col Ampliación Granada • 5325-9000*

9 Lucha Libre
This entertaining "sport" features costumed wrestlers wearing masks *(see p56)*.

10 Acapulco Cliff Divers
Acapulco's most famous attraction in which young men leap from a 130-ft (40-m) cliff into sea below. ✪ *La Quebrada*

Band performing at the Festival de México, Centro Histórico

🔟 Festivals and Events

1 Día de los Reyes Magos

Three Kings' Day, or Epiphany on January 6, is the traditional gift giving day, when families gather to celebrate. In the days leading up to it, children have their photos taken with the Three Kings, send their gift wish list aloft through balloons, and help select the sweet cakes, *rosca de reyes*, which are served on this day.

Semana Santa procession

2 Semana Santa

The "Holy Week" from Palm Sunday to Easter Sunday is one of the most important festivals in Mexico. It combines Catholic tradition with pre-Hispanic festivities. Over a million people gather at Iztapalapa, south of downtown Mexico City, for the annual Passion Play. Good Friday is a day of plays and costumed processions.

3 Holy Saturday

On the Saturday between Good Friday and Easter Sunday, holy vigils and solemn masses are held in many churches. Later, participants gather outside as huge effigies of Judas and other evil forces, are burned signifying the triumph of good over evil.

4 Feria de la Flor más Bella del Ejido

Xochimilco celebrates the arrival of spring, its floriculture, and the ancient Aztec goddess of flowers with a week of festivities in late March or early April. Music in the streets, an abundance of colorful flowers, and family events typify this small-town style festival. One of the highlights is a competition for the most beautifully decorated *trajinera*, or flat boat. ☎ 5676-8879

5 Festival de México

Two weeks of fabulous concerts and special cultural events are held in traditional performing arts venues, historic *palacios,* and in the streets, parks, and plazas of Centro Histórico during March or early April. ☎ http://festival.org.mx

6 Día de la Madre

Mother's Day in Mexico is on May 10 and is a joyful occasion. The restaurants are filled with family celebrations. Mothers receive bouquets of roses as presents and are serenaded by *mariachis (see p57).*

7 Defense of Mexico and Fall of Tenochtitlán

Festivities commemorate the valiant defense of Tenochtitlán by the Aztecs, led by Cuauhtémoc, against the Spaniards. Brilliantly costumed *concheros* perform ritual pre-Hispanic dances on August 13 at the Plaza de las Tres Culturas *(see p95).*

Día de los Muertos

The Day of the Dead in Mexico is a two day celebration to honor deceased relatives and ancestors. Families invite the dead to visit by creating elaborate altars decorated with candy skulls, flowers, and the favorite foods of the departed. It is believed that deceased children return on November 1st. The next day the dead adult relatives and ancestors visit.

Día de Nuestra Señora de Guadalupe

Throughout December pilgrims from across the Americas arrive at Villa de Guadalupe to honor their patron saint and Mexico's beloved Our Lady of Guadalupe. Thousands time their arrival for December 12, the Feast Day of the Virgin of Guadalupe, to attend the mass and thank the Virgin. Pilgrims often complete their journey to the Villa de Guadalupe on their knees.

Feast Day celebrations, Villa de Guadalupe

Las Posadas

Christmas processions and plays re-enacting the story of Mary and Joseph seeking lodging and the nativity scene are nightly events throughout the city in the days leading up to Christmas, December 16–24. Candle- and lantern-lit processions fill the streets heading to churches for mass. The Zócalo is decorated with lights and major performance venues hold special events.

Top 10 Public Holidays

New Year's Day (Jan 1)

December 31 sees parties all night. Traditionally, colored eggshells filled with confetti are tossed into the air.

Constitution Day (Feb 5)

A National Holiday which commemorates the new Constitution of 1917.

Natalicio de Benito Juárez (Mar 21)

Mexico's national hero and great reformer President Benito Juárez's *(see p39)* birthday is a national holiday.

Easter Thursday and Good Friday

Holy Thursday (March/April) is a traditional day of worship at churches. Passion Plays are held on Good Friday.

Labor Day (May 1)

Parades by workers are held in the streets.

Cinco de Mayo (May 5)

Commemorates the 1862 Battle of Puebla, where the Mexican army defeated the invading French.

Independence Day (Sep 16)

On the evening before, the President issues the cry of independence and rings the Freedom Bell at the Zócalo. A parade through Centro is held on this day.

Día de la Raza (Oct 12)

Celebrates Colombus' discovery of the New World.

Revolution Day (Nov 20)

Marks the anniversary of the 1910 Revolution *(see p39)*.

Christmas (Dec 25)

Midnight masses are followed by festivities on Christmas.

Left **Pyramid of the Sun, Teotihuacán** Center **Taxco** Right **La Parroquia, San Miguel de Allende**

10 Excursions

1 Teotihuacán
Once the greatest city in Mesoamerica, the ancient ruins form one of the world's biggest and most impressive archeological zones. Visitors can climb the third largest pyramid in the world, stroll through ancient palaces, and see fabulous ancient murals *(see pp32–3)*.

Iglesia de San Francisco Javier, Tepotzotlán

2 Tepotzotlán
The highlight of this mountain town with its pretty plaza and cobblestone streets is the magnificent Iglesia de San Francisco Javier. Next to the church is the Jesuit college which houses the Museo Nacional del Virreinato displaying colonial and religious art. ⊛ *27 miles (44 km) N of Mexico City • 5876-2326 • Bus tour and taxi • 9am–5:45pm Tue–Sun • Adm, free Sun • www.tepotzotlan.gob.mx*

3 Tula
Tula, the capital of the Toltec nation, rose to power in the 10th century, after the fall of Teotihuacán. The most important ruin here is the Pyramid of Tlahuizcalpantecuhtli (Pyramid of the Morning Star). Four towering Atlanteans, the famous monumental carved stone warriors, crown the pyramid. Other ruins include the Wall of Serpents, ball courts, and the columns of the Burnt Palace. ⊛ *53 miles (85 km) N of Mexico City • (773) 732-1183 • Bus tour • 10am–5pm Tue–Sun • Adm • www.inah.gob.mx*

4 Taxco
This picturesque colonial mountain town with steep, narrow cobblestone streets is most famous for its talented silversmiths, historic buildings, and the fabulous Baroque church Iglesia de Santa Prisca. The Spaniards first mined a wealth of silver here, and Taxco was established as the center for silversmiths in the 1930s. Today, silver shops surround the town's main plaza. ⊛ *106 miles (170 km) SW of Mexico City • (762) 622-0798*

Atlante de Tula

5 Cuernavaca
Year-round spring-like weather and a convenient location near Mexico City have attracted the wealthy and powerful to this lovely colonial town for centuries. Cortés built his fortress-like residence, Palacio de Cortés, here in 1522. The town center features a cathedral built in the 1520s and nearby there are two lovely plazas. Palacio de

Cortés and Jardín Borda were used by Emperor Maximilian I and his wife Carlota as a retreat. Both are open to the public from Tuesday to Sunday. ✆ *56 miles (90 km) S of Mexico City • (777) 314-3920 • www.morelostravel.com*

Puebla

Puebla is famous for its beautiful colonial buildings decorated with hand-painted Talavera tiles. Founded in 1531, the city is nestled between the mountains Popocatépetl, La Malinche, and Iztaccíhuatl. It is also known for its colonial churches, fine museums, and numerous boutiques offering exquisite Mexican handicrafts and pottery. ✆ *81 miles (130 km) E of Mexico City • (222) 246-2044, (1-800) 087-1980 • www.puebla.gob.mx*

Museo de Santa Rosa, Puebla

Valle de Bravo

Wild and beautiful, this area attracts nature lovers and extreme sports enthusiasts. From December to February the Monarch Butterfly Reserve draws many visitors, who come to witness the amazing sight of millions of the brilliant orange butterflies cloaking the forests. ✆ *91 miles (147 km) W of Mexico City • (1-800) 696-9696 • www. valledebravo.com.mx*

Parque Nacional Iztaccíhuatl-Popocatépetl

The second and third highest peaks in Mexico are in a pine-forested wilderness area with excellent hiking and mountain biking trails. Paseo de Cortés is another popular place for hiking and mountain biking with excellent views of the volcanoes. ✆ *45 miles (72 km) SE of Mexico City • (597) 978-3829 • 7am–9pm daily • Adm*

San Miguel de Allende

This charming mountain town is a Mexican National Historic Monument with a lovely city center, a shady plaza surrounded by shops and cafés, and a brilliant Neo-Gothic church, La Parroquia. ✆ *174 miles (280 km) NW of Mexico City • (415) 152-9600 ext. 203*

Acapulco

With sandy beaches and the warm Pacific Ocean, Acapulco is the perfect place to unwind. The 4-mile (7-km) wide bay offers a selection of beaches for relaxing, family fun, or partying. ✆ *190 miles (300 km) SW of Mexico City • (744) 484-2216 • www. visiteacapulco.com*

Valle de Bravo is popular with power boaters, sailors, hikers, mountain bikers, hang gliders, and parasailers

AROUND TOWN

MEXICO CITY'S TOP 10

Left **Antiguo Colegio de San Ildefonso** Center **Museo Nacional de Arte** Right **Palacio de Bellas Artes**

Centro Histórico

THIS HISTORIC CENTER OF MEXICO CITY, *one of the largest cities in the world, has been a vibrant hub of culture, religion, and politics since the days of the Aztecs. An organized grid of streets extends from the Zócalo, the city's political and social gathering place, leading to incredible churches and palaces, some of which have been turned into fine museums. Other colonial buildings now house boutique hotels, shops, and restaurants. Although it is a busy, noisy, and thriving part of a modern metropolis, you can still find tranquil plazas and quiet old courtyards away from the hustle and bustle.*

Sights

1. Zócalo
2. Palacio Nacional
3. Templo Mayor
4. Catedral Metropolitana
5. Palacio de Bellas Artes
6. Parque Alameda Central
7. Museo Franz Mayer
8. Antiguo Colegio de San Ildefonso
9. Museo Nacional de Arte
10. Museo SHCP in the Palacio del Arzobispado

Catedral Metropolitana, Palacio Nacional, and Zócalo

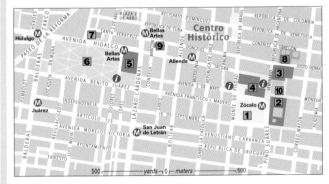

Preceding pages **The colorful domes of Museo del Carmen in San Ángel**

Zócalo

Plaza de la Constitución, also known as Zócalo, was one of the city's main market areas from the days of Tenochtitlán. In the 1860s, Emperor Maximilian I banned merchants and created a Parisian park, with tree-lined walkways and benches. Following the Mexican Revolution the plaza was cleared of all the trees, grass, and ornamentation. The plaza is today the gathering place for social and political causes. 🔌 *Monte de Piedad* • *Map Q3*

Military ceremony at the Zócalo

Palacio Nacional

This huge government edifice extends along the length of the Zócalo. Cortés built his palace on the site of the Aztec Emperor Moctezuma II's castle in 1563. The current palace was constructed in 1693 following fires in 1659 and 1692 which destroyed much of the earlier building. Emperor Maximilian I modified the architecture introducing European flair. President Calles added the third floor in 1926. Today, most visitors come to view the brilliant murals of Diego Rivera, especially his *Epic of the Mexican People*, which surrounds the central staircase *(see pp14–15)*.

Templo Mayor

This was once the largest and most important temple in the ceremonial complex at the heart of the Aztec empire, until the Spanish destroyed it after their conquest and used the rubble for their own construction. In 1978, city workers digging near the Catedral Metropolitana discovered a carved stone disk, over 10 ft (3 m) in diameter, that enabled archeologists to determine the location of the temple. A major archeological project ensued covering several city blocks. Today, visitors can follow a winding walkway through the excavated ruins and visit the excellent museum which displays many of the artifacts recovered here *(see pp16–17)*.

Catedral Metropolitana

The largest cathedral in the Western Hemisphere, it took 240 years to complete. This is reflected in the dazzling array of Baroque and Neo-Classical styles. Built on soft, marshy soil the cathedral was sinking until engineers used a variety of techniques to stabilize it. The cathedral still has a visible tilt, but a huge pendulum hung from the dome marks the slow movement towards the perpendicular. An exceptional collection of paintings, religious furnishings, and glittering altars adorn the interior *(see pp12–13)*.

Altar Mayor, Catedral Metropolitana

A huge Mexican national flag is raised and lowered every day with much military ceremony from a towering pole in the Zócalo

Museo Franz Mayer

Palacio de Bellas Artes

Built between 1905 and 1934, this stunning performing arts venue presents a fascinating blend of architectural styles. The dazzling Beaux Arts white Italian marble exterior features ornate domes, columns, and European sculptures and carvings. The interior is a superb Art Deco extravaganza, with red marble columns, black marble floors, classic light fixtures, and brass details. Four stories of Art Deco columns, balconies, and grillwork house a spectacular theater, famous murals, fine gift and book shops, and traveling art exhibitions *(see pp20–21)*.

Parque Alameda Central

The oldest park in the city was established on the site of an Aztec market by the order of Viceroy Don Luis de Velasco in 1590. It was named after the poplar trees planted there. With shade-giving trees and walking paths, the park provides some tranquil respite from the bustle of the city. Fountains and statues adorn the park, including a bronze figure of Neptune, God of the Sea. ❧ *Av Juárez, Angela Peralta, Av Hidalgo and Dr Mora • Map N2*

Museo Franz Mayer

Fabulous decorative arts from the 16th through 19th century are displayed in this former hospital building built in the 18th century. The features of the old building, the archways, carved wood doors, and frescos, have been incorporated into the design of the display areas which tastefully augment the collection of beautiful everyday decorative objects from Mexico, Europe, and Asia. ❧ *Av Hidalgo 45 • Map N2 • 5518-2266 • 10am–5pm Tue–Fri, 11am–7pm Sat & Sun • Adm • www.franzmayer.org.mx*

Antiguo Colegio de San Ildefonso

Built as a small Jesuit college in 1588, the building is now best known as the birthplace of the modern muralist movement.

Antiguo Colegio de San Ildefonso

Diego Rivera painted his first mural, *The Creation,* here in 1922–3. The walls inside have works of early muralists such as José Clemente Orozco, David Alfaro Siqueiros, and Fernando Leal. ❧ *Justo Sierra 16 • Map Q2 • 5702-2991 • 10am– 5:30pm Tue–Sun (to 7:30pm Tue) • Adm for Murals only, General, Exhibition, and Murals tours; free Tue • www. sanildefonso.org.mx*

The outstanding Ballet Folklórico performs at the Palacio de Bellas Artes on Wednesdays and Sundays

Museo Nacional de Arte

This stunning collection has over 3,000 works by great artists including Miguel Cabrera, José María Velasco, and Diego Rivera. Arranged chronologically, the exhibits focus on the art of New Spain, National Mexican Art, and the modern art that evolved during and after the Revolution. The Neo-Classical building is fabulous, with a double staircase, ornamental ironwork, and beautiful ceiling paintings by Mariano Coppedé (1839–1920).

§ *Tacuba 8 • Map P2 • 5130-3400 • 10:30am–5:30pm Tue–Sun • Adm, free Sun • www.munal.com.mx*

Detailed carvings, Museo Nacional de Arte

Museo SHCP in the Palacio del Arzobispado

This intriguing museum displays art accepted by the Finance Secretariat in lieu of tax payments. Both famous and little known artists are on display. Juan Correa's *Nacimiento de la Virgen*, Miguel Cabrera's *Don Juan Antonio*, and Diego Rivera's painting of his San Ángel studio are showcased here. Recent tax years' collections are kept in a separate gallery. § *Moneda 4 • Map Q2 • 3688-1259 • 10am–5:30pm Tue–Sun • Adm • www.museosdemexico.org*

Museo SHCP in the Palacio del Arzobispado

An Alameda Central Stroll

Morning

Have breakfast in the lovely courtyard of the **Casa de los Azulejos** *(see p44)*, now a **Sanborns Restaurant** *(see p73)*, admiring the fountain, and the exquisite mural by Orozco. Across the street is the late Baroque **Iglesia y Ex-Convento de San Francisco** *(see p48)* and next door is the towering **Torre Latinoamericana** *(see p71)*. Take the elevator to the 44th floor for an exceptional view of the city. Next visit the grand **Palacio de Bellas Artes** *(see pp20–21)* to explore the fabulous Beaux Arts building with its Art Deco interior. Catch the brilliant murals by Rivera, Siqueiros, Orozco, and Tamayo in the second and third floor porticoes. Lunch at the dining room of the *palacio*.

Afternoon

Walk through lovely **Parque Alameda Central** *(see p46)*, to the west of the Palacio de Bellas Artes, and enjoy the park's fountains. Next proceed across Av Hidalgo to the **Museo Franz Mayer** which houses a great collection of decorative arts. Then head east on Av Hidalgo, across Tacuba into the **Palacio Postal** *(see p71)*. The Post Office is famous for its stunning staircase and architecture. Then cross Tacuba and walk on to Plaza Manuel Tolsá to the famous statue **El Caballito** or *The Little Horse (see p75)* by Manuel Tolsá (1757–1816). Spend the rest of the afternoon at **Museo Nacional de Arte** *(see pp26–7)*.

Left **Museo Interactivo de Economía** Center **Museo del Ejército** Right **Museo de Arte Popular**

🔟 Small Museums

Museo del Ejército
The exhibits of this museum include military armaments and the armor of the Spanish conquistadors. ◐ *Filomeno Mata 6 • Map P2 • 5512-3215 • 10am–6pm Tue–Sat, 10am–4pm Sun • Free*

Museo Interactivo de Economía
Interactive and easy-to-understand exhibits about economics are this museum's attraction. ◐ *Tacuba 17 • Map P2 • 5130-4600 • 9am–6pm Tue–Sun • Adm • www.mide.org.mx*

Museo de Arte Popular
Folk art from across Mexico is showcased in this exceptional museum in a lovely Art Deco building. ◐ *Revillagigedo 11 (entrance by Independencia) • Map N2 • 5518-1648 • 10am–6pm Tue–Sun (to 9pm Wed) • Adm • www.map.df.gob.mx*

Museo Mural Diego Rivera
This museum houses Diego Rivera's famous mural, *Dream of a Sunday Afternoon in the Alameda Central (see p51).*

Museo de la Charrería
The Mexican culture and traditions of the *charrería*, or horsemen, are presented in this museum. ◐ *Isabel la Católica 108 • Map P4 • 5709-5032 • 10am–7pm Mon–Fri • Free*

Museo José Luis Cuevas
A large collection of works by renowned Mexican artist José Luis Cuevas is displayed here, along with works of other artists. ◐ *Academia 13 • Map R2 • 5522-0156 • 10am–6pm Tue–Sun • Adm, free Sun • www.museojoseluiscuevas.com.mx*

Casa de la Primera Imprenta
This building housed the first printing press in the Americas. A science museum today, it has a model of the press *(see p40).*

Secretaría de Educación Pública
Diego Rivera painted over 100 murals that cover the walls of this building *(see p50).*

Museo de la Caricatura
A fascinating collection of Mexican cartoons are displayed in this museum. ◐ *Donceles 99, Col Centro • Map Q2 • 5704-0459 • 10am–6pm daily • Adm*

Museo de la Ciudad de México y Estudio de Joaquín Clausell
This museum has maps, paintings, and early photographs of Mexico City. Upstairs is the former studio of Mexican painter Joaquín Clausell. ◐ *Pino Suárez 30 • Map Q3 • 5542-0083 • 10am–5:30pm Tue–Sun • Adm, free Wed • www.cultura.df.gob.mx*

Left **Hemiciclo a Juárez** Right **Plaza de Santo Domingo**

🔟 Best of the Rest

Iglesia de la Profesa
An early Baroque façade, a Mexican Baroque interior, and a Neo-Classical altarpiece by Manuel Tolsá are highlights of this church *(see p49)*.

Casa de los Azulejos
This 18th-century aristocratic residence with an inner courtyard and exquisitely decorated rooms is sheathed in lovely decorative blue tiles *(see p44)*.

Hemiciclo a Juárez
This striking monument was built in honor of President Benito Juárez in 1910. Guillermo de Heredia designed the open semicircle. Italian sculptor Lazzaroni created the statue and the supporting sculptures. 🔊 *Next to Parque Alameda Central on Av Juárez • Map N2*

Plaza Ciudadela and Mercado de Artesanías de la Ciudadela
The largest handicrafts and souvenir market in the downtown area offers a dazzling array of textiles, crafts, and artwork *(see p53)*.

Mercado San Juan
Artisans gather in this indoor market, offering traditional and artistic handcrafted wares including fine jewelry, ceramics, and handwoven textiles *(see p53)*.

Torre Latinoamericana
Take the elevator to the 44th floor of this slender glass skyscraper for an astounding view of the city. 🔊 *Eje Central 2 • Map P2 • 5518-7423 • 9am–10pm daily • Adm • www.torrelatino.com*

Templo de la Enseñanza
This narrow church with its intricately carved late-Baroque façade has nine grandiose ultra-Baroque altarpieces *(see p48)*.

Plaza de Santo Domingo
This plaza, important in the colonial era, is surrounded by austere colonial buildings and the lovely Templo de Santo Domingo on the north *(see p48)*.

Laboratorio Arte Alameda
This museum, located in the former convent of San Diego, presents contemporary art through temporary exhibits, screenings, and events. 🔊 *Dr Mora 7, Col Centro • Map N2 • 5510-2793 • 9am–5pm Tue–Sun • Adm, free Sun • www.artealameda.bellasartes.gob.mx*

Palacio Postal
Completed in 1907, this stunning *palacio*, the main post office, has an amazing central staircase and an ornate interior. 🔊 *Tacuba and Eje Central Lázaro Cárdenas • Map P2 • 5510-2999 • 8am–8pm daily (to 4pm Sat & Sun) • www.palaciopostal.gob.mx*

Left **Librería Gandhi** Center **Mexican wall-hanging** Right **Arte Mexicano Para el Mundo**

Shopping

1 Arte Mexicano para el Mundo

Reasonably priced, quality Mexican handicrafts are displayed in this pretty colonial building. ⊗ *Monte de Piedad 11, Col Centro • Map Q3 • 4160-4176 • www.arte-mexicano.com.mx*

2 Librería Gandhi

This bookstore offers titles in Spanish, and some in English. They also have a good selection of music CDs. ⊗ *Av Juárez 4, Col Centro • Map N2 • 2625-0606 • www.gandhi.com.mx*

3 Dulcería de Celaya

Since 1874 this charming store has specialized in traditional Mexican sweets such as candied nuts and crystallized fruits. ⊗ *Av 5 de Mayo 39, Col Centro • Map P2 • 5521-1787 • www.dulceriadecelaya.com*

4 Palacio de Bellas Artes Shops

The first floor lobby offers three shops, an excellent bookstore, a music shop, and a small gift shop *(see pp20–21)*.

5 Museo de Arte Popular

The large shop located in the lobby of the Museo de Arte Popular offers bright and colorful Mexican folk art and handicrafts *(see p70)*.

6 Nacional Monte de Piedad

The large showrooms of the National Pawnshop are filled with glittering antique and contemporary jewelry. ⊗ *Monte de Piedad 7, Col Centro • Map Q2 • 5278-1700 • 8:30am–6pm Mon–Fri, 8:30am–1pm Sat • www.montepiedad.com.mx*

7 La Europea

This chain of liquor stores has one of the best selections of tequilas and wine in the city. ⊗ *Ayuntamiento 21, Col Centro • Map P3 • 5512-6005 • www.laeuropea.com.mx*

8 Pastelería Ideal

This bakery is famous for its wedding and birthday cakes, which are often complex and colorful works of art. ⊗ *Av 16 de Septiembre 18, Col Centro • Map P3 • 5130-2970 • www.pasteleriaideal.com.mx*

9 Perfumes y Esencias Fraiche

Perfumes and essences are made to order, with perfumers hand-blending the scents. ⊗ *16 de Septiembre 52, Col Centro • Map P2 • (1800) 337-2424 • www.fraiche.com.mx*

10 Catedral Vendors

In front of the Catedral Metropolitana, vendors offer religious relics, prayer cards, and rosaries. Near Templo Mayor, vendors present Mexican crafts *(see pp12–13)*.

Price Categories

For a three course meal
for one with half a bottle
of wine (or equivalent
meal), taxes, and
extra charges.

$	under 150 pesos
$$	150–250 pesos
$$$	250–350 pesos
$$$$	350–450 pesos
$$$$$	over 450 pesos

Above **Bar la Ópera**

🔟 Places to Eat

1 La Casa de las Sirenas
Dine on modern Mexican cuisine, such as *cilantro soup* and *mole poblano*. Downstairs, there is a cantina and tequila bar. ✆ *Guatemala 32 • Map Q2 • 5704-3345 • www.lacasadelassirenas.com.mx • $$$*

2 Los Girasoles
This restaurant offers traditional Mexican cuisine including pre-Hispanic dishes. *Salsas*, *tortilla* soup, tamarind *mole*, and duckling in blackberry sauce are popular. ✆ *Tacuba 8 and 10, Plaza Manuel Tolsá • Map P2 • 5510-0630 • www. restaurantelosgirasoles.com • $$$$*

3 Bar la Ópera
This historic cantina offers a great Mexican menu, along with opulent red booths, polished woodwork, a gleaming long bar, and a bullet hole in the ceiling, courtesy of Pancho Villa. ✆ *Cinco de Mayo 10 • Map P2 • 5512-8959 • $$$*

4 Sanborns in Casa de los Azulejos
Always busy, this favorite meeting spot offers traditional Mexican comfort food, as well as international favorites, in an opulent colonial setting. ✆ *Madero 4 • Map P2 • 5510-9613 • $$*

5 Café Tacuba
Excellent traditional Mexican entrées like *Oaxacan tamal* and *enchiladas Tacuba* are on offer at a reasonable price. ✆ *Tacuba 28 • Map P2 • 5518-4950 • www. cafedetacuba.com.mx • $$*

6 Casino Español
Traditional Spanish cuisine where favorites like *paella* and baked goat are served. ✆ *Isabel la Católica 31 • Map P3 • 5521-8894 • 1–6pm daily • $$*

7 Puro Corazón
Trendy *nouvelle* Mexican cuisine such as *mole poblano* and *arrachera* beef are served here. ✆ *Monte de Piedad 11 • Map Q2 • 5518-0300 • www.arte-mexicano.com.mx • $$$*

8 Hostería de Santo Domingo
The place serves classic Mexican cuisine such as *chiles en nogada* and *mole poblano*. ✆ *Belisario Domínguez 72 • Map Q2 • 5526-5276 • www. hosteriadesantodomingo.com.mx • $$*

9 Coox Hanal
This popular place serves Yucatecan specialties such as *cochinita pibil* (slow-roasted pork). Watch out for the fiery *salsas*! ✆ *Isabel la Católica 83, 3rd Floor • Map P4 • $*

10 El Cardenal
Come to this family favorite for such dishes as *flor de maguey* (cactus flower) and *escamoles* (ant eggs). ✆ *Palma 23 (betw. Av 5 de Mayo & Madero) • Map P3 • 5521-8815 • $$$*

Small restaurants may only accept cash; vegetarians might want to ask about cooking oil as animal fat is frequently used

73

Left **Detail, Monumento a la Revolución** Center **El Caballito** Right **Monumento a la Independencia**

Paseo de la Reforma and Zona Rosa

PASEO DE LA REFORMA WAS BUILT *in 1865 at the direction of Emperor Maximilian I on the lines of Paris's Champs-Élysées. Today this broad boulevard is one of the city's showpieces, a major thoroughfare with gleaming monuments of marble and gold punctuating the grand traffic circles, the glorietas. It offers pedestrians a beautiful promenade of shady trees, flower gardens, bronze statues, and park benches. Zona Rosa, an eclectic area of sidewalk cafés, fine restaurants, mid-size hotels, diverse shopping venues, and pulsating nightlife, is on the south of the boulevard.*

🔟 Sights

1. Monumento a la Revolución
2. Museo Nacional de la Revolución
3. Museo Nacional de San Carlos
4. El Caballito (The Little Horse)
5. Monumento de Colón
6. Monumento a Cuauhtémoc
7. Zona Rosa
8. Monumento a la Independencia, El Ángel
9. Fuente de la Diana Cazadora
10. Museo Casa de Carranza

El Ángel

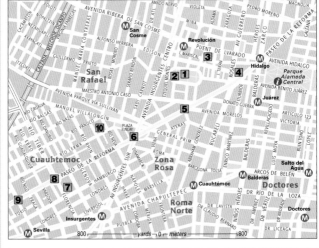

800 ⌐————yards—0—meters————¬ 800

Take a stroll down the promenade or ride the Turibus to see the monuments in the glorietas (traffic circles)

1 Monumento a la Revolución

This massive monument to the Revolution dominates the Plaza of the Republic. Construction of the building began during President Porfirio Díaz's reign, and was to have housed the legislature. Following the bloody revolt, the unfinished shell was repurposed to memorialize the Revolution and serve as a mausoleum for the remains of some of the uprising's heroes, including Pancho Villa, Venustiano Carranza, Francisco I. Madero, Plutarco Elías Calles, and Lázaro Cárdenas. ◈ *Plaza de la República, Col Cuauhtémoc • Map L2*

Museo Nacional de la Revolución

2 Museo Nacional de la Revolución

This excellent museum in the basement of the Monumento a la Revolución portrays Mexican history from 1867 to the Revolutionary constitution of 1917. The exhibits focus on the people and events of this period, telling the story through the use of photographs, newspaper headlines announcing Revolution, historic documents, furnishings, displays of the personal belongings of key figures, guns and rifles used in battle of 1914, and a reward poster for Pancho Villa dated March 9, 1916. ◈ *Plaza de la República, Col Tabacalera • Map L2 • 5546-2115 • 9am–5pm Tue–Sun • Adm, free Sun • www.cultura.df.gob.mx*

Rear façade, Museo Nacional de San Carlos

3 Museo Nacional de San Carlos

This impressive Neo-Classical building designed by Manuel Tolsá houses a most impressive collection of European art. It displays paintings from the 15th to the early 20th century and includes notable oils from the Flemish, French, Italian, and Spanish schools. Highlights include oils by Rubens, sketches by Goya, and sculptures by Rodin. ◈ *Av Puente de Alvarado 50, Col Tabacalera • Map M2 • 5566-8342 • 10am–6pm Wed–Mon • Adm, free Sun • www.mnsancarlos.com*

4 El Caballito (The Little Horse)

This monumental bright yellow metallic sculpture by renowned Mexican artist Sebastián was dedicated in 1992. Considered one of his finest works, the statue makes a dramatic statement and dominates the plaza it stands in with the skyscraper known as the Torre del Caballito behind it. The modern statue represents the head of a horse and replaced a classical sculpture by Manuel Tolsá of Charles IV on horseback. It had stood there for 127 years, until 1979 when the street was altered. Both sculptures are known as *El Caballito*. ◈ *Paseo de la Reforma and Rosales • Map M2*

Around Town – Paseo de la Reforma and Zona Rosa

Walk of the Reform

Emperor Maximilian I named the road "Causeway of the Empress" for his wife. After the Republic was restored, it was renamed Paseo de la Reforma (Walk of the Reform). The road was transformed, and under Porfirio Díaz the major monuments were placed in the *glorietas* (traffic circles), and 36 statues of national heroes were placed along the road.

Monumento de Colón

Explorer Christopher Columbus is commemorated in this monument inaugurated in 1877. Created in France by artist Carlos Cordier, the statue was donated to the city by Don Antonio Escandón. Seated on the red limestone pedestal below Colón (Colombus) are four bronze statues of Friar Diego de Deza who supported his project, Friar Juan Pérez de Marchena, Friar Bartolomé de las Casas, defender of the native cause, and Friar Pedro de Gante. 🜪 *Paseo de la Reforma glorieta at Av Morelos and I. Ramírez • Map L3*

Monumento a Cuauhtémoc

Cuauhtémoc was the last Aztec emperor and led the defense of Tenochtitlán against the Spaniards until he was captured during the final battle at Tlatelolco on August 13, 1521. This powerful monument was designed by Francisco Jiménez and the bronze statue of Cuauhtémoc holding his spear aloft was sculpted by Miguel Noreña. The bas-reliefs on the base depict the torture of Cuauhtémoc by the Spanish. 🜪 *Paseo de la Reforma glorieta at Insurgentes Sur • Map K3*

Monumento a Cauhtémoc

Zona Rosa

Once a trendy neighborhood of first-class hotels and restaurants, sidewalk cafés, and boutiques, Zona Rosa's elegant past has been overrun by the tawdry nightlife now found here. Visitors should exercise caution if they are going out in the evening. 🜪 *Paseo de la Reforma, Niza, Av Chapultepec and Varsovia • Map K4*

Zona Rosa

Monumento a la Independencia, El Ángel

Widely referred to as El Ángel for the Winged Victory at the top, the glorious monument to Mexican Independence was inaugurated in 1910 to celebrate Mexico's first century of independence from Spain. The steel column covered with the names of heroes is 118 ft (36 m) high. The Winged Victory, by artist Enrique Alciati, is of bronze covered with gold and stands 22 ft (6.7 m) high. The four bronze statues at the corners of the base of the column symbolize Law, Justice, War, and Peace. 🜪 *Paseo de la Reforma, glorieta at Florencia • Map J4*

9 Fuente de la Diana Cazadora

Fuente de la Diana Cazadora

A magnificent statue of Roman goddess Diana the Huntress adorns the fountain in the westernmost *glorieta* on the Paseo de la Reforma. Sculpted by John Olaguíbel, the bronze statue weighs over a ton. The voluptuous nude Diana created much debate and controversy in 1942, and finally the artist covered her loins with a bronze covering, which remained in place until 1967. The stone fountain was designed by architect Vicente Mendiola.

⊛ *Paseo de la Reforma glorieta at Río Rhin • Map G3*

10 Museo Casa de Carranza

Venustiano Carranza was a Mexican Revolutionary leader and President of the Republic from 1917–20. He was later executed in Puebla on May 7, 1920. He lived in this 1908 building, inspired by French architecture, for the last six months of his life. Memorabilia from Carranza's life, furnishings, art, and a library of the Constitution of 1917 fill 13 exhibition rooms. The museum has an extensive photographic collection which covers the tumultuous period of the Mexican Revolution. It includes photos of the legislative council that approved Mexico's present constitution on February 5, 1917.

⊛ *Río Lerma 35, Col Cuauhtémoc • Map K3 • 5546-6494 • 9am–5pm Tue–Sat, 10am–5pm Sun • Free • www.museocasadecarranza.mx*

Paseo de la Reforma by Foot and Turibus

Morning

🕐 Begin from **El Caballito** *(see p75)*, at the corner of Av Juárez and board the **Turibus** *(see p104)* to the **Monumento a la Revolución** *(see p75)* north of the Reforma. Hop off at stop #13 to visit **Museo Nacional de la Revolución** *(see p75)* and also the **Museo Nacional de San Carlos** *(see p75)*. Back on the bus, take a top deck seat to view the skyline and the **Monumento de Colón** and **Monumento a Cuauhtémoc** at the *glorietas*. A majestic palm tree occupies the next *glorieta*. To the north is the **Bolsa Mexicana de Valores** *(see p45)* with its glass dome between two high-rise glass buildings. Get off at stop #15 for **Monumento a la Independencia**. Walk south across Reforma into the shopping and café district of Zona Rosa. On the right is **Mercado Insurgentes** *(see p52)* and on the left is **Plaza del Ángel** *(see p78)*. Just ahead is a great café, **Konditori** *(see p79)*, where you can stop for lunch.

Afternoon

Return to the Turibus stop #15. Take a seat upstairs and watch for the Roman goddess Diana, the huntress, in the final *glorieta* standing atop **Fuente de la Diana Cazadora**. Step off the bus at stop #16 and head to the 52nd floor of **Torre Mayor** *(see p45)* for an incredible view of Mexico City. Downstairs, the Torre Mayor also has trendy shops, boutiques, and cafés. Stop for a cup of café con leche, a special Mexican coffee.

Left **Antique shop, Plaza del Ángel** Right **Via Spiga**

Shopping

Fonart
One of the best stores to shop for Mexican handicrafts – everything from ceramics to woven baskets are available here. ◈ Paseo de la Reforma No. 333, Col Juárez • Map L3 • 5093-6000 • www.fonart.gob.mx

Plaza del Ángel
This attractive plaza houses some 30 antique shops selling an amazing selection of fine antiques, including porcelain, oil paintings, furniture, and silver. ◈ Londres 161, Col Juárez • Map H3

Mercado Insurgentes
One of the best, and most fun, places to shop for silver jewelry, sculpture, and tableware is this Zona Rosa marketplace. With some 200 booths, the selection of jewelry is outstanding. ◈ Londres 160 and Liverpool 161 • Map J4

Via Spiga
The latest handcrafted Italian leather boots, shoes, purses, and bags of excellent quality are available here. ◈ Hamburgo 136, Col Juárez • Map H3 • 5207-9224

Hevart's Galería de Arte
This gallery sells colorful, classically inspired, Mexican-styled oil paintings of landscapes and still-lifes of fruits and flowers. Fine marble or bronze sculptures of family scenes are also available. ◈ Entrance from Amberes, NH Mexico City, Col Juárez • Map H3 • 5228-9928 extn. 1666

Plaza Parque Reforma 222
This multilevel shopping mall features brand-name stores, a cinema, and several international restaurants. ◈ Paseo de la Reforma 222 • Map K3 • www.reforma222.com

Artesanias El Luna
Traditional Mexican crafts – baskets, ceramics, jewelry, and blankets – can be found here. ◈ Hamburgo 88B, Col Juárez • Map K4

Plaza la Rosa
This lively shopping center in the center of Zona Rosa offers dozens of brand-name clothing stores. ◈ Between Amberes and Génova, Col Juárez • Map H3

Sanborns
This department store offers a restaurant, ATM, pharmacy, gift items, and a books, periodicals, and CD section. ◈ Paseo de la Reforma 45 • Map H3 • 5705-5722 • www.sanborns.com.mx

El Péndulo
In addition to a wide range of books, CDs, and DVDs, this store offers an attractive café/ wine bar with live music at weekends *(see opposite)*.

Price Categories

For a three course meal for one with half a bottle of wine (or equivalent meal), taxes, and extra charges.

$	under 150 pesos
$$	150–250 pesos
$$$	250–350 pesos
$$$$	350–450 pesos
$$$$$	over 450 pesos

Above **Les Moustaches**

TOP 10 Places to Eat

1 Gaudí
Fine Spanish cuisine, including medallions of steak in sherry, and red snapper in cider, is served in this elegant dining room. The pleasant café in the lobby serves breakfasts, light meals, and a Mexican buffet. ◈ *Imperial Hotel, Paseo de la Reforma 64 • Map L3 • $$$*

2 Manhattan Deli
This attractive restaurant serves New York-style deli meals in an upscale but relaxed atmosphere. ◈ *Hotel María Isabel Sheraton • Map J4 • 5242-5555 extn. 3701 • $$$*

3 Tezka
Creative Basque-influenced cuisine blends sweet and savory flavors throughout the menu of this place. The extensive wine list complements the entrées. ◈ *Hotel Royal, Zona Rosa • Map H3 • 5228-9918 • Closed Sun • $$$$$*

4 El Bajio
Chef Carmen Tititia prepares some of the best traditional Mexican food in the city. Try the *carnitas* (roast pork) or the duck in black *mole*. ◈ *Paseo de la Reforma 222 • Map K3 • 5511-9124, 5511-9117 • Closes at 11pm daily (8pm Sun) • $$$$*

5 Fonda el Refugio
Authentic cuisine from the major regions of Mexico is served in this charming restaurant. The daily specials include *mole poblano* and *albóndigas en chile chipotle*. ◈ *Liverpool 166, Col Juárez • Map H3 • 5525-8128 • $$*

6 Café Milano
Richly flavored Italian cuisine and international favorites are on the menu in this café at the Room Mate Valentina *(see p114)*.

7 Konditori
This café is famous for its flaky Danish pastries and Scandinavian cuisine. Sandwiches and other entrées are also available here. ◈ *Génova 61, Col Juárez • Map K4 • 5511-0722 • www.konditori.com.mx • $$$*

8 Les Moustaches
Excellent French cuisine and wine are served here. ◈ *Río Sena 88, Col Cuauhtémoc • Map H2 • 5525-1265 • www.lesmoustaches.com.mx • $$$$$*

9 Cielo Rojo
Savor the excellent traditional Mexican cuisine served here with tequila, margaritas, *mezcal*, or *pulque*. ◈ *Génova 70, Col Juárez • Map K4 • 5525-1196 • $$$*

10 Café El Péndulo
Large platters of *huevos péndulo*, omelets, soups, and salads are served here. ◈ *Hamburgo 126, Col Juárez • Map H3 • 5208-2327 • www.pendulo.com • $$*

Left **Bosque de Chapultepec** Center **Museo Rufino Tamayo** Right **Performers from Veracruz**

Chapultepec and Polanco

FOR CENTURIES AN EXCLUSIVE RETREAT *for the leaders of ancient Mexico, Bosque de Chapultepec was turned into a public park by President Lázaro Cárdenas in the 1930s. Today, it seems, almost everyone in the city heads to the park on weekends to enjoy the lakes, woods, zoo, and museums. Vendors lining the pathways contribute to the festive air. Just north of the park, Polanco is home to many of the city's wealthiest residents. It also has high-end stores, fine restaurants, pleasant cafés, and boutique shops.*

Sights

1 Museo Nacional de Antropología
2 Castillo de Chapultepec
3 Museo de Arte Moderno
4 Museo Rufino Tamayo
5 Zoológico de Chapultepec
6 Monumento a los Niños Héroes
7 Museo de Historia Natural
8 Bosque de Chapultepec
9 Fuente de Tláloc
10 Papalote Museo del Niño

Lago Mayor, Bosque de Chapultepec

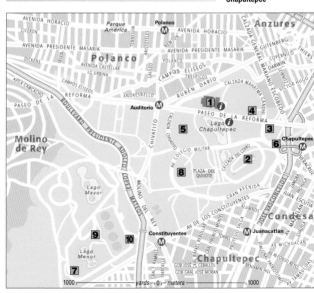

1 Museo Nacional de Antropología

This internationally renowned anthropology museum show-cases, in a series of halls, original artifacts from pre-Hispanic Mexico discovered at archeological sites throughout the country. The magnificent 180-ton monolith of Tláloc, God of Rain, stands near the entrance. Inside, an impressive central courtyard is dominated by a modern, 36-ft (11-m), intricately decorated pillar. It symbolically represents the pre-Hispanic past and the scientific and technological future. It alone supports a 275-ft (84-m) long concrete canopy (see pp8–9).

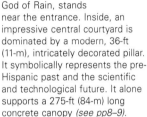

Chacmool, Museo Nacional de Antropología

2 Castillo de Chapultepec

Located atop the highest point in Bosque de Chapultepec, the enormous castle with its fortress-like walls dominates the Mexico City skyline. The personal residence of Emperor Maximilian I, President Porfirio Díaz, and other Mexican presidents until 1939, the castle is now the head-quarters of the National History Museum with two sections – the Alcázar and the Castillo (see p43).
⬡ Section 1, Bosque de Chapultepec • Map E4 • 4040-5214 • 9am–4:30pm Tue–Sun • Adm, free Sun • www.mnh.inah.gob.mx

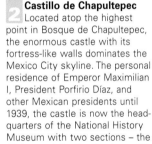

Castillo de Chapultepec

3 Museo de Arte Moderno

Excellent modern paintings, sculpture, and photography from some of the best known 20th-century Mexican artists are part of the permanent collection housed in this Pedro Ramírez Vásquez-designed building. Frida Kahlo's huge painting, Las Dos Fridas (The Two Fridas), is on display here. Oil paintings by the great muralists are well represented, as are works by José Luis Cuevas (b. 1934) and Manuel Felguérez (b. 1928).
⬡ Paseo de la Reforma and Gandhi, Bosque de Chapultepec • Map F3 • 5211-8331 • 10am–5:30pm Tue–Sun • Adm, free Sun • www.conaculta.gob.mx/mam

Museo de Arte Moderno

4 Museo Rufino Tamayo

This magnificent collection by internationally recognized modern artists was accumulated by renowned Mexican artist Rufino Tamayo. Tamayo and his wife Olga donated the museum and their collection in 1981. More than 160 artists, international as well as Mexican, are represented including Salvador Dalí, Max Ernst, William de Kooning, Andy Warhol, Francisco Toledo, José Luis Cuevas, Sebastián, and of course Rufino Tamayo. Selected works from the permanent collection are exhibited, along-side temporary visiting exhibi-tions. ⬡ Paseo de la Reforma and Gandhi, Bosque de Chapultepec • Map E3 • 5286-6519 • 10am–6pm Tue–Sun • Adm, free Sun • www.museotamayo.org

Voladores de Papantla

The flying men from Veracruz present their traditional ritual near the entrance to the Museo Nacional de Antropología. Five men climb to the top of a 75-ft (23-m) pole. As one plays music and dances, the other four take turns to gracefully slide off the platform with a rope tied to one leg, gradually swirling upside down until each reaches the ground.

Zoológico de Chapultepec

Famous for its giant pandas, the zoo is home to more than 250 different species. Here, popular animals such as tigers and elephants live alongside rare native animals, such as the Mexican hairless dog. ◎ Section 1, Bosque de Chapultepec • Map D3 • 5553-6263 • 9am–4:30pm Tue–Sun • Free • www.chapultepec.df.gob.mx

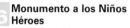
Elephant, Zoológico de Chapultepec

Monumento a los Niños Héroes

This striking marble monument at the main entrance to Bosque de Chapultepec honors the six young cadets who fought valiantly during the US invasion of 1847, defying orders to retreat. The last cadet standing, wrapped the Mexican flag around himself and jumped off the battlements. ◎ Section 2, Bosque de Chapultepec • Map B6

Monumento a los Niños Héroes

Museo de Historia Natural

Museo de Historia Natural

The displays of this museum are ideal for children to learn about the natural world. A small planetarium offers exhibits on the creation of the universe, the solar system, and earth. A dinosaur skeleton dominates the center of the Evolution of Life Hall. Three stuffed polar bears are the highlights of the Life on Earth Hall. There is also a section on the Natural History of Mexico. ◎ Section 2, Bosque de Chapultepec • Map B6 • 5515-6304 • 10am–5pm Tue–Sun • Adm, free Tue • www.sma.df.gob.mx/mhn

Bosque de Chapultepec

One of the largest, prettiest, and most visited urban parks in the world, Bosque de Chapultepec is loved by Mexicans and visitors alike. Many visitors discover the park while visiting the Museo Nacional de Antropología or the spectacular hilltop Castillo de Chapultepec which houses the Museo Nacional de Historia. The park offers miles of paved walkways that lead through woods, past lakes, into lovely gardens, and connect to many more significant museums and attractions. There are lakeside restaurants, picnic spots with tall, shady trees, shops, and places to rent paddleboats (see pp22–3).

Zoológico de Chapultepec also has an extensive collection of birds, including a large walk-through aviary of Mexican species

9 Fuente de Tláloc

This whimsical multi-hued horizontal mosaic sculpture of a running Tláloc, the Aztec God of Rain, was designed by Diego Rivera in 1952. A favorite with children, the fountain spreads in front of a small building called El Cárcamo that was once part of the city's water system. Inside, Diego Rivera painted huge murals with beautiful flowing designs venerating water and the workers who built the system that brings water into Mexico City. ⊗ *Section 2, Bosque de Chapultepec • Map C5*

Papalote Museo del Niño

10 Papalote Museo del Niño

"Not touching is forbidden" is the motto at this fascinating children's museum. All of the 250 activities are interactive and focus on art, science, and technology. A creative complex of three brightly colored cubic, spherical, and triangular shaped buildings, designed by architect Ricardo Legorreta, houses the museum. The building also has an IMAX theater. The museum adds new exhibits frequently, often collaborating with corporate donors to include state-of-the-art equipment and activities. Two of the most popular exhibits are the flight simulator and the interactive traditional crafts area. ⊗ *Section 2, Bosque de Chapultepec • Map C6 • 5237-1773 • 10am–8pm daily (to 11pm Thu) • Adm • www.papalote.org.mx*

Museum Highlights Walk

Morning

🕐 To the right of the entrance to **Bosque de Chapultepec** is the **Museo de Arte Moderno**. Turn left on the road that leads up to the **Castillo de Chapultepec** *(see p43)*. When you reach the **Casa de los Espejos** *(see p25)* take a tram to the top of the hill. The road curves past the **Museo del Caracol** *(see p24)*, which highlights major moments in Mexican history. At the top of the hill enter the Castillo and go straight to the **Alcázar Section** of the **Museo Nacional de Historia** *(see p43)*. Explore the opulent rooms of the former **President's Mansion**, walk up the **Staircase of the Lions**, and visit the **Garden of the Keep** *(see p25)*. Head back to the museum's **Castillo Section** *(see p43)* and look at the murals in the main staircase and the first floor before visiting the gift shop.

Afternoon

Descend the hill and follow a sidewalk lined with many vendors – you may want to buy a cold bottled drink – to **Lago de Chapultepec** *(see p23)*. Turn right toward the **Museo Nacional de Antropología** *(see pp8–9)* and follow the signs. After you enter the museum go into the courtyard and turn left down the stairs for lunch in the excellent café. Spend the rest of the day exploring the fabulous halls of this renowned anthropological museum. Be sure to see the **Mexica Hall** *(see pp10–11)* at the end of the courtyard, and the **Teotihuacán Hall**.

Around Town – Chapultepec and Polanco

Left **Fashion stores, Avenida Presidente Masarik** Center **Talavera ceramics** Right **Shops, Polanco**

Shops and Galleries

1 Galería Enrique Guerrero
This gallery presents the works of masters such as José Clemente Orozco. Contemporary artists are also promoted.
⌾ *Horacio 1549 • 5280-2941*
• www.galeriaenriqueguerrero.com

2 Galería Lopez Quiroga
The gallery offers a great selection of paintings, drawings, sculpture, ceramics, and jewelry.
⌾ *Aristóteles 169, Col Polanco • Map C1*
• 5280-1710 • www.lopezquiroga.com

3 Ginocchio Galería
Specializing in modern and contemporary works, this gallery displays a range of Mexican and international art. ⌾ *Arquímedes 175, Col Polanco • Map D1 • 5254-8813*
• www.ginocchiogaleria.com

4 Galería Juan Martín
The gallery promotes contemporary Mexican art. It has prints by Manuel Bravo, acrylics by Roger Von Gunten, and ceramics by Francisco Toledo.
⌾ *Dickens 33B, Col Polanco • 5280-0277*
• www.arte-mexico.com/juanmartin

5 Galería Oscar Román
The gallery presents works of famous and emerging contemporary Mexican artists. ⌾ *Julio Verne 14, Col Polanco • 5280-0436*
• www.galeriaoscarroman.com.mx

6 Tienda MAP
This store of the Museo de Arte Popular in the Centro Histórico *(see p70)* stocks the most refined collection of Mexican handicrafts in the city.
⌾ *Emilio Castelar 22 (at Temístocles), Col Polanco • Map D2 • www.tiendamap.com*

7 Frattina
This boutique offers the very best Mexican and international designer collections and accessories for women. ⌾ *Av Presidente Masarik 420, Col Polanco • 5281-4028*
• www.frattina.com.mx

8 Tane
Exceptional Mexican silver designs are on sale in this boutique shop. ⌾ *Av Presidente Masarik 430, Col Polanco • 5282-6200*
• www.tane.com.mx

9 Pasaje Polanco
Boutique shops surround a lovely courtyard just south of Av Presidente Masarik, selling everything from shawls to toys.
⌾ *Polanco, off Oscar Wilde*

10 Avenida Presidente Masarik
This avenue is lined with the best-known fashion and accessory stores including Cartier, DKNY, and Tiffany. ⌾ *Av Presidente Masarik, Col Polanco • Map C2*

Hacienda de los Morales

Price Categories

For a three course meal for one with half a bottle of wine (or equivalent meal), taxes, and extra charges.

$	under 150 pesos
$$	150–250 pesos
$$$	250–350 pesos
$$$$	350–450 pesos
$$$$$	over 450 pesos

TOP 10 Places to Eat

1 Hacienda de los Morales
Elegant international and Mexican dining in a charming, 16th-century colonial hacienda. ⊗ *Vázquez de Mella 525, Col Del Bosque • 5283-3054 • Coat and tie for dinner, reservations required • $$$$$*

2 Dulce Patria
Star chef Marta Chapa puts a creative and eclectic spin on traditional Mexican cuisine. Impeccable presentation and service. ⊗ *Anatole France 100, Col Polanco • 3300-3999 • Closed Sun dinner • $$$$$*

3 Pujol
Visit this stylish restaurant for dishes such as ceviche in coconut milk and fish cooked in ashes of *chile ancho.* ⊗ *Francisco Petrarca 254, Col Polanco • 5545-4111 • Closed Sun • $$$$$*

4 Bello Puerto
Reasonable prices, colorful beach decor, and lively music draw a young, attractive crowd to this popular seafood restaurant. ⊗ *Julio Verne 89, Col Polanco • 5281-0980 • Closes at 11pm daily (7pm Sun) • $$$*

5 Los Panchos
This popular restaurant near the park specializes in *carnitas* (roast pork); indeed, they are said to be the best in the city. It is also worth trying the handmade *tortillas,* the *salsas,* and the *aguas frescas* (fresh fruit drinks). ⊗ *Tolstoi 9, Col Anzures • Map F3 • 5254-5430 • Closes at 10pm daily (8pm Sun) • $$*

6 Au Pied de Cochon
Sublime French cuisine, including classic onion soup, is served round the clock at this bistro in the Presidente Inter-Continental Hotel *(see p112).* ⊗ *Reservations recommended • $$$$*

7 Thai Gardens
Authentic, exotic Thai cuisine is served in this elegant restaurant. ⊗ *Calderón de la Barca 72, Col Polanco • 5281-3850 • $$$$*

8 Izote
Cookbook author Patricia Quintana prepares creative Mexican food with traditional pre-Hispanic ingredients. ⊗ *Av Presidente Masarik 513, Col Polanco • 5280-1671 • Reservations recommended • $$$$$*

9 Rincón Argentino
Large platters of excellent beef are grilled to order. The decor is casual Argentina ranch. ⊗ *Av Presidente Masarik 177, Col Polanco • 5254-8744 • $$$$$*

10 Meridiem
The restaurant's extensive menu provides great choice. ⊗ *Lago Mayor, Section 2, Bosque de Chapultepec • 5273-3599 • $$$$*

Small restaurants may only accept cash; vegetarians might want to ask about cooking oil as animal fat is frequently used

Left **El Bazar de Sábado Restaurant** Right **Museo del Carmen**

Coyoacán and San Ángel

ONCE SMALL COLONIAL TOWNS, *both Coyoacán and San Ángel have retained their charm although they are engulfed by the ever-expanding Mexico City. Both are tranquil oases that offer glimpses of traditional Mexican life, with green park-like plazas, cobblestone streets, flower gardens, and old colonial mansions. In 1519, Cortés made Coyoacán his base during the siege of Tenochtitlán. Dominican and Carmelite friars moved into San Ángel after the Spanish conquest. In the 20th century the area's quiet beauty attracted artists and celebrities including Diego Rivera, Frida Kahlo, and political refugee León Trotsky. Visitors flock here to visit the former homes and studios of these famous people and savor the towns' artistic environment. They shop for paintings and crafts, enjoy the sidewalk cafés, boutique shops, and museums.*

🔟 Sights

1. Museo Frida Kahlo
2. Plaza Hidalgo
3. Museo Nacional de las Intervenciones
4. Museo León Trotsky
5. Bazar de Sábado
6. Ex-Convento e Iglesia del Carmen
7. Museo Casa Estudio Diego Rivera y Frida Kahlo
8. Museo Nacional de la Acuarela
9. Museo de Arte Carrillo Gil
10. Museo Soumaya

Jardín del Centenario, Plaza Hidalgo

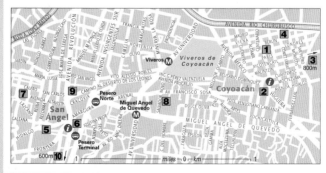

In the Náhuatl language Coyoacán means "Place of the Coyotes"

Museo Frida Kahlo

1 Museo Frida Kahlo
This vibrant blue house is where Frida Kahlo was born and spent most of her life creating her greatest works. A self-taught painter, she developed a unique style here that blended realist and surrealist elements. The house is filled with personal belongings, paintings, and the favorite artworks of Frida and her husband, Diego Rivera. Frida's studio has her easel and paintbrushes, the bedroom displays her signature Mexican regional clothing and jewelry, and the cheery kitchen is filled with Mexican pottery. ✪ *Londres 247, Col Coyoacán • Map X1 • 5554-5999 • 10am–5:45pm Tue–Sun • Adm • www. museofridakahlo.org*

2 Plaza Hidalgo
At one end of this bustling plaza stands the Iglesia de San Juan Bautista. The church's elegant interior features a 17th-century Baroque altarpiece. Across the plaza is the 18th-century municipal building. Murals depicting local history are in the attached chapel. Across the Calle Carrillo Puerto is Jardín del Centenario *(see p47)*. Here stands the famous Fountain of Coyoacán. ✪ *Calles Carrillo Puerto, Caballo Calco and B. Domínguez • Map X2*

3 Museo Nacional de las Intervenciones
Museo Nacional de las Intervenciones is located within the complex of El Antiguo Convento Churubusco. It chronicles the invasions of Mexico following its independence from Spain. Highlighted here is the Spanish invasion of 1829, the French invasion of 1838–9, the US invasion of 1846–7, the French invasion of 1862–7 as well as incursions by the USA in 1914 and 1916. There are displays of documents, military artifacts, uniforms, and stories of the heroes and villains.
✪ *Calle 20 de Agosto s/n, Col San Diego Churubusco • 5604-0699 • 9am–6pm Tue–Sun • Adm • www.inah.gob.mx*

4 Museo León Trotsky
Often referred to as the "Little Fortress", this was the home of Russian revolutionary León Trotsky from 1939 until his assassination here on August 20, 1940. The house remains the way it was on the day he was murdered. The desk in his study is covered with his papers, pens, a calendar, and a magnifying glass. Also seen are his books and typewriter. Bullet holes from an earlier attempt on his life riddle the walls, and worn Mexican rugs lie on the floors. His ashes are interred in the peaceful courtyard. ✪ *Av Río Churubusco 410 • Map X1 • 5554-0687 • 10am–5pm Tue–Sun • Adm*

Museo León Trotsky

Weekends at the Plaza Hidalgo are festive, with musicians and mime artists entertaining the crowd

Around Town – Coyoacán and San Ángel

La Malinche

Mystery surrounds La Malinche, the indigenous woman who was Cortés' mistress, translator, and trusted negotiator. It is believed that she was sold into slavery after her father's death. Whether she was a victim or an opportunist is debated, but Mexicans often view her as a traitor to her people. She lived in Coyoacán with Cortés' son.

Bazar de Sábado

This festive Saturday-only shopping event is housed in an old colonial mansion. Dozens of tastefully decorated booths displaying exquisite decorative and functional art fill the rooms around the courtyard. Intricate silver jewelry, hand-embroidered clothing, papier-mâché figures, hand-carved and painted wood-work, and ceramics are on offer. The mansion's courtyard is home to the El Bazar de Sábado Restaurant (see p93). ⊗ Plaza San Jacinto 13 • Map S3 • 10am–7pm Sat

Ex-Convento e Iglesia del Carmen

Built for Carmelite monks in the 17th century, three beautiful mosaic-tiled domes adorn the church. The next-door museum, Museo del Carmen, offers displays of exceptional religious art. A basement crypt discovered

The domes of the Museo del Carmen

in 1914 contains the mummified bodies of priests, nuns, and nobility. On the top floor is a chapel with a Baroque altar. ⊗ Av Revolución 4, San Ángel • Map T3 • 5616-1504 • 10am–5pm Tue–Sun • Adm for museum, free Sun

Frida Kahlo's studio

Museo Casa Estudio Diego Rivera y Frida Kahlo

Built by fellow muralist, friend, and architect Juan O'Gorman in 1931–2, the complex has two buildings joined by a second-floor walkway. The larger white studio was Diego Rivera's, where he painted many of his best known oils. The smaller blue one was Frida Kahlo's when she lived here with Rivera. Diego's has been left unaltered, with some of the paintings still standing on easels. ⊗ Calle Diego Rivera and Altavista • Map S2 • 5550-1518 • 10am–6pm Tue–Sun • Adm • www.estudiodiegorivera.bellas artes.gob.mx

Museo Nacional de la Acuarela

This internationally renowned museum was founded by cele-brated artist Alfredo Guati Rojo and his wife. It has a permanent exhibit on the history of water-color in Mexico, an international section, and galleries displaying contemporary Mexican art. Works by the likes of Pastor Velázquez, Manuel M. Ituarte, Eduardo Solares, and Leandro Izaguirre adorn the gallery walls. ⊗ Salvador Novo 88 • Map V2 • 5554-1801 • 10am–6pm daily • Free • www.acuarela.org.mx

Museo de Arte Carrillo Gil

The museum's permanent collection of early 20th-century Mexican masters includes paintings by José Clemente Orozco, David Alfaro Siqueiros, Diego Rivera, Gunther Gerzso, Wolfgang Paalen, and others. The collection was assembled by Dr. Álvar and Carmen Carrillo Gil and is housed in a bright, modern three-story building in San Ángel. The museum is noted for its exceptional temporary exhibits featuring Mexican and international contemporary art.

Av Revolución 1608 • Map T2 • 5550-6260 • 10am–6pm Tue–Sun • Adm, free Sun • www.museodeartecarrillogil.com

Museo de Arte Carillo Gil

Museo Soumaya

This private museum features Latin America's largest collection of sculptures in marble, bronze, and terracotta by famed French sculptor Auguste Rodin (1840–1917). The collection includes *Burghers of Calais*, *The Kiss*, *Eve*, *The Eternal Spring*, and many other fine sculptures. Other collections include 18th- and 19th-century Mexican portraits, the Art of New Spain, and works by international artists such as Edgar Degas, Paul Gauguin, and Camille Claudelle. The museum also displays temporary exhibits by renowned Mexican and international artists.

Av Revolución and Río Magdalena, Plaza Loreto • 5616-3731 • 10:30am–6:30pm Wed–Mon (to 8:30pm Fri & Sat) • Adm • www.soumaya.com.mx

A Stroll Through Coyoacán

Morning

Begin at the **Museo Nacional de la Acuarela** located on Salvador Novo, south of Avenida Francisco Sosa. After viewing the excellent watercolors, walk back to Avenida Francisco Sosa along one of the prettiest cobblestone streets of Coyoacán with its many attractive old colonial mansions and the charming yellow Church of Santa Catarina built in the middle of 17th century. Cross the street into the garden of the cultural center, Casa de la Cultura Jesús Reyes Heroles (No. 202). Farther along is the **Jardín del Centenario** (see p47). View the Fountain of the Coyotes. Move to the adjacent Plaza Hidalgo and admire the interior of the Iglesia de San Juan Bautista. Explore the area around the plaza. Lunch at trendy **Los Danzantes** (see p93).

Afternoon

Head north on Allende for three blocks to **Mercado de Coyoacán** (see p52) and soak in the sights, sounds, and smells in this pretty market where colorful arrays of fresh fruits and vegetables, *piñatas*, toys, and crafts are on sale amid the tantalizing smell of Mexican food. Carry on to Londres to visit the **Museo Frida Kahlo** (see p89) where the famous artist was born, lived, and painted. Continue on to Viena and turn right to visit **Museo León Trotsky** (see p89). Head back to Plaza Hidalgo for some of Coyoacán's renowned ice cream at **Helados Siberia** (see p93).

Left **Bust of Diego Rivera** Center **Museo Dolores Olmedo** Right **Courtyard, Museo Frida Kahlo**

Frida Kahlo, Diego Rivera, and Mexican National Art

1 National Art
After the Civil War ended in 1920, President Álvaro Obregón decided that education and a new form of distinctly Mexican art would help heal the wounds of the war and unite the country.

2 The First Murals
As part of the policy, the government comissioned Diego Rivera in 1922. He painted *The Creation*, in the Antiguo Colegio de San Ildefonso *(see p68)*.

3 Artistic Syndicate
The Revolutionary Syndicate of Technical Workers, Painters, and Sculptors was formed in 1922 with the intent to focus on public art, rather than easel painting.

4 Diego Rivera (1886–1957)
A master painter, he was trained in Mexico and Europe, and was known for his bright, bold figures and visual story telling.

5 Frida Kahlo (1907–54)
A self-taught artist, Frida created paintings that captured her emotions and political ideals in a unique style combining realist and surrealist elements.

6 Diego Rivera and Frida Kahlo Romance
Individually they created vastly different art, but together their tumultuous relationship came to embody 20th-century Mexican art.

7 Homes and Studios
Frida lived and painted in her Coyoacán home, now Museo Frida Kahlo *(see p89)*, for much of her life. After their marriage Rivera built his San Ángel studio, now Museo Casa Estudio Diego Rivera y Frida Kahlo *(see p90)*. They lived there for a time, and this is where he did most of his painting. After Frida died, Diego built another studio nearby, now known as the Museo Diego Rivera Anahuacalli *(see p97)*.

8 Museo Dolores Olmedo
A friend and patron of Diego Rivera, Dolores Olmedo Patiño collected his work and made a museum of her estate *(see p95)*.

9 Frida Kahlo's Most Famous Works
Frida Kahlo's *Two Fridas* is at the Museo de Arte Moderno *(see p83)* and *Self-Portrait with a Monkey* and *The Broken Spine* are at Museo Dolores Olmedo.

10 Diego Rivera's Most Famous Works
The most visited mural is *Epic of the Mexican People* in the Palacio Nacional *(see pp14–15)*. *Man the Controller of the Universe* in the Palacio de Bellas Artes *(see pp20–21)* is a re-creation of his Rockefeller Center mural. *Dream of a Sunday Afternoon in the Alameda Central* is in Museo Mural Diego Rivera *(see p51)*.

Museo Dolores Olmedo has the largest collection of easel paintings by Diego Rivera and Frida Kahlo in the world

Price Categories

For a three course meal for one with half a bottle of wine (or equivalent meal), taxes, and extra charges.

$	under 150 pesos
$$	150–250 pesos
$$$	250–350 pesos
$$$$	350–450 pesos
$$$$$	over 450 pesos

Los Danzantes

🔟 Places to Eat

1 Helados Siberia
This legendary ice-cream shop has an excellent selection of flavors. ◎ *Plaza Jardín del Centenario 3, Col Coyoacán • Map X2 • Cash only • $*

2 Taberna de León
Chef Monica Patiño prepares Mexican and international specialties in this romantic restaurant located in a converted paper factory. ◎ *Altamirano 46, Plaza Loreto, Col San Ángel • 5616-3951 • Closed Sun dinner • $$$$*

3 Cantina La Coyoacana
This traditional family cantina with its bullfighting decor serves Mexican specialties in a circa-1932 mansion with an antique bar, stained-glass windows, and a great ambience. ◎ *Higuera 14, Col Coyoacán • Map X2 • 5658-5337 • Mon–Sat • $$*

4 Fonda San Ángel
Mexican specialties with exceptional sauces are served in this cozy restaurant. ◎ *Plaza San Jacinto 3, Col San Ángel • Map T3 • 5550-1641 • www.fondasanangel.com.mx • $$$$*

5 Los Danzantes
Come to this stylish, intimate restaurant for contemporary Mexican fusion cuisine with Oaxacan flavors and a creative twist. ◎ *Plaza Jardín Centenario 12, Col Coyoacán • Map W3 • 5658-6451 • www.losdanzantes.com • $$$$*

6 San Ángel Inn
Housed in an old Carmelite monastery, this fine restaurant offers both formal and casual dining. ◎ *Diego Rivera 50, Col San Ángel • Map S2 • 5616-2222 • www.sanangelinn.com • $$$$$*

7 Entre Vero
This attractive and informal bistro serves Uruguayan specialties. ◎ *Jardín Centenario 14-C, Col Coyoacán • Map W2 • 5659-0066 • $$$$*

8 Tasca Manolo
This restaurant's menu is international eclectic, with traditional Spanish entrées and Mexican favorites. ◎ *Av de la Paz 32, Col San Ángel • Map T2 • 5550-9191 • $$$$$*

9 Cluny
Savory French entrées and dessert crepes attract diners to this restaurant. ◎ *Av de la Paz 57, Col San Ángel • Map T2 • 5550-7350 • www.cluny.com.mx • $$*

10 El Bazar de Sábado Restaurant
This café is housed in the courtyard of the Bazar de Sábado (see p90). ◎ *Plaza San Jacinto 13, Col San Ángel • Map S3 • 5550-0772 • 10am–1pm Sat brunch, 1–6pm Sat lunch • www.fondasanangel.com.mx • $$$$*

Small restaurants may only accept cash; vegetarians might want to ask about cooking oil as animal fat is frequently used

93

Left **Tenayuca** Center **Canal, Xochimilco Floating Gardens** Right **Plaza de las Tres Culturas**

Greater Mexico City

BEYOND THE TRADITIONAL AREAS *brimming with attractions in Mexico City, there are many other fascinating sites away from the center and visitable by taxi or bus tour. Every year millions visit Villa de Guadalupe, the holiest shrine in Mexico. Locals and visitors alike flock to Xochimilco to tour the ancient canals, while art lovers enjoy the nearby Museo Dolores Olmedo. Weekends and holidays are perfect times for excursions to the cool, refreshing pine-forested mountains of the National Parks. Ecological parks offer varied outdoor activities in the heart of nature.*

🔟 Sights

1. Villa de Guadalupe
2. Plaza de las Tres Culturas
3. Tenayuca and Santa Cecilia Acatitlán
4. Museo Dolores Olmedo
5. Xochimilco Floating Gardens
6. Parque Ecológico de Xochimilco
7. Parque Nacional Desierto de los Leones
8. Parque Nacional los Dinamos
9. Parroquia de San Bernardino de Siena
10. Museo Diego Rivera Anahuacalli

Parque Nacional Desierto de los Leones

Nueva Basílica, Villa de Guadalupe

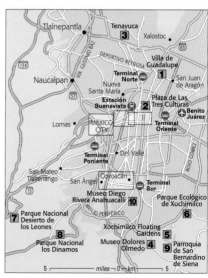

Capilla del Cerrito, Villa de Guadalupe

Villa de Guadalupe

Mexico's holiest Catholic shrine is dedicated to Our Lady of Guadalupe, the beautiful dark-skinned image of the Virgin that appeared to Juan Diego in 1531 and left an imprint of her image on his cloak. The cloak is displayed in the Nueva Basílica. There are numerous chapels, basilicas, and holy sites here, each one commemorating an aspect of this holy site. The Basílica Antigua, with its beautiful Baroque façade and twin towers, housed the image of Guadalupe from 1709 until the Nueva Basílica was consecrated in 1976 (see pp30–31).

Plaza de las Tres Culturas

Tlatelolco was the site of the largest Aztec commercial trading center. The Spanish conquistadors destroyed the Aztec palaces, temples, and ceremonial center making way for the plaza and the Church of Santiago. Much of the ruins, including the main pyramid with its twin temples, have been excavated. Modern buildings surround the plaza, giving rise to the name which means "plaza of three cultures," for the Aztec, colonial, and modern era structures. ◈ Eje Central & Ricardo Flores Magón • Map B2 • Ruins 9am–6pm Tue–Sun • Adm free

Tenayuca and Santa Cecilia Acatitlán

These two ancient pyramids located near each other in the north of Mexico City make it possible to visit both archeological sites in a single taxi trip. The oldest, Tenayuca was built in the 11th century before the Aztecs arrived in the valley. The pyramid was enlarged every 52 years, six times in all, and twin staircases lead to the temples on the top. The second pyramid, Santa Cecilia Acatitlán, dates from 1300–1521, and was used to worship the sun god Huitzilopochtli and the rain god Tláloc. The temple at the top of the pyramid has been carefully and authentically reconstructed, and visitors can climb the staircase to explore the building (see p41).

Museo Dolores Olmedo

Housed in the gracious 17th-century Hacienda La Noria is the largest private collection of easel works by renowned Mexican artists Diego Rivera and Frida Kahlo. Philanthropist Dolores Olmedo Patiño was Diego Rivera's friend, patron, and occasional model, and she collected 145 of his works. The Frida Kahlo collection includes 25 of her works. ◈ Av México 5843 Col La Noria, Xochimilco • Map B4 • 5555-1221 • 10am–6pm Tue–Sun • Adm, free Tue • www.museodoloresolmedo.org.mx

Museo Dolores Olmedo

Tlalpan

Located to the south of the National University is the old colonial neighbourhood of Tlalpan. The central plaza with pleasant gardens and shady paths is bordered by the pretty 16th-century Baroque Iglesia de San Agustín de las Cuevas, and several fine restaurants and shops. The narrow streets are lined with 17th- and 18th-century mansions.

Xochimilco Floating Gardens

Popular with both locals and tourists, many come to the floating gardens to glide leisurely in *trajineras* (flat-bottomed barges) through the shallow waters of the ancient Aztec canals lined with flower-festooned nurseries and homes. Decorated with brightly colored flower motifs, the barges are available for rent by the hour *(see pp28–9)*.

Parque Ecológico de Xochimilco

Parque Ecológico de Xochimilco

This 740-acre (300-hectare) park was created to help preserve and maintain Xochimilco's canals and floating gardens and is protected by UNESCO. *Trajineras* provide boat trips through the natural areas to see native and cultivated flora and various species of birds; walking paths also curve through the park. There is a visitor center, a museum, and shows that explain how the Aztecs built the floating islands *(see pp28–9)*.

Parque Nacional Desierto de los Leones

Mexico's first National Park is a beautiful mountainside forest of oak and pine, with numerous streams and the remains of a fascinating Carmelite monastery to explore. The monastery dates from 1611, and the name, "Desert of the Lions," refers to the biblical Elijah who lived isolated in the wilderness. Beautiful flower gardens surround the monastery. There are many recreational options, such as hiking and biking trails and on weekends there are trail horses for rent. It is a good idea to speak with a ranger before leaving the well-traveled areas of the park, as sometimes theft is a problem in less popular sections. A restaurant housed in the monastery offers Mexican favorites. ◈ *Camino al Desierto de los Leones • Map A4 • Taxi • 9am–6pm daily • Adm • Monastery open 10am–6pm Tue–Sun*

Parque Nacional los Dinamos

Popular with nature lovers, this wooded expanse borders the ravine of the Magdalena River. Favorite activities here include walking, hiking, and biking. Horses are often available for hire on weekends and holidays, and there are plenty of picnic spots. The park also offers the best rock climbing in the area, with walls of varying difficulty reaching as high as 100 ft (30 m). There are several different rock formations requiring a variety of climbing techniques. Weekends and holidays are the best time to visit. If you plan to explore the less-frequented areas of the park it is advisable that you first speak with one of the park's rangers. ◈ *Magdalena Contreras • Map A4 • 9am–5pm daily • Adm free*

9 Parroquia de San Bernardino de Siena

Flower-filled gardens surround this graceful church. Ornate doorways lead to one of Mexico's last surviving 16th-century altarpieces. This magnificent *retablo* has paintings by Baltazar de Echave and sculptures by Luis de Arciniega. A unique feature of this church is the pre-Hispanic skulls mounted on the side walls, with a sign reminding parishioners how to make a good confession. ◈ *Pino and Violeta, Xochimilco • Map C4 • Adm free*

Museo Diego Rivera Anahuacalli

10 Museo Diego Rivera Anahuacalli

Designed by Diego Rivera to house his spectacular collection of thousands of pre-Hispanic Mexican artifacts, this huge, black, volcanic rock building incorporates Mayan and Toltec design elements. The collection includes figurines from Tlatilco, masks from Teotihuacán, and the sculptures of four Aztec deities, the goddess of corn and the gods of wind, fire, and rain. Rivera died before the building was completed, but his two-story studio is decorated as he planned to use it. Large sketches of some of his murals hang on the walls. ◈ *Calle Museo 150, Col San Pablo Tepetlapa • Map B3 • 5617-4310 • Taxi • 11am–4:30pm Wed–Sun (till 4pm Fri) • Adm; all visits are guided • www.anahuacallimuseo.org*

A Walk Through Colonia Condesa

Afternoon

🕐 Take the **Turibus** *(see p104)* and get off at stop #3, or take a taxi to Av Michoacán *(Map F6)*. This beautiful residential neighborhood has tree-shaded avenues and Art Deco houses, and is a favorite with writers, artists, and musicians. This trendy area boasts cafés that are popular with the city's young professionals.

🍴 Try **La Buena Tierra** *(see p99)* for excellent organic fare, or the nearby **Don Asado** *(see p99)* for meat dishes and pizzas. After lunch, continue along Av Michoacán and cross Av México *(Map H5)*, entering the pretty **Parque México** *(see p46)* and walk to the Fountain of the Water Jugs which has a statue of a nude woman holding two ceramic jugs with water flowing from them. Once part of Mexico's premier horse racing track, this oval park features wide shady paths, lush landscaping, and beautiful fountains. Exit the park at the northeast corner on to Av México. Continue past the lovely 14-story Art Deco masterpiece Edificio Basurto by architect Francisco J. Serrano and completed in 1945. Admire the lovely, dome-shaped white Art Deco fountain in Plaza Popocatépetl *(Map H5)*, designed by José Gómez Echeverría in 1927. Walk to the right, almost all the way around the circular plaza, exiting on to Av México. Continue on to Av Michoacán, passing Art Deco buildings and then head back to the Turibus stop where you can have dessert or snacks at one of the many sidewalk restaurants.

Left **Parque Hundido** Right **Avenida Insurgentes**

Insurgentes Sur

Avenida Insurgentes
When the university was built in the far south of Mexico City in the 1950s, this broad avenue was created to link it with the rest of the city. Avenida Insurgentes today stretches for 28 miles (45 km) and Insurgentes Sur, the southern stretch, is a happening area. ◎ Map K4

Roma
Colonia Roma, with its tree-lined streets and varied architecture, was developed in the early 20th century. The area, popular with wealthy residents, is known for its contemporary art galleries and cafés. ◎ Map G4

Casa Lamm
This popular culture center, bookstore, art gallery, and restaurant is housed in a 1911 mansion. ◎ Av Álvaro Obregón 99, Col Roma • Map K6 • 5525-1332 • Art Gallery 10am–6pm daily; Library 9am–7pm Mon–Sat, 10am–7pm Sun; Bookstore 11am–8pm Mon–Sat, 10am–7pm Sun • www.casalamm.com.mx

Condesa
Colonia Condesa, with pleasant, tree-lined streets and parks, is home to many artists and creative people. There are also many trendy restaurants here. ◎ Map F5

World Trade Center
This glass skyscraper has a revolving restaurant, Bellini, on the 45th floor. ◎ Montecito 38, Col Nápoles • 9000-6000 • www.torrewtc.com

Polyforum Siqueiros
Conceived and designed by the master-muralist David Alfaro Siqueiros, this futuristic building integrates modern architecture, sculpture, and art forms. It also showcases sculpted murals. ◎ Av Insurgentes Sur 701 Col Nápoles • Map B3 • 5536-4520 • 9am–6pm • Adm • www.polyforumsiqueiros.com.mx

Plaza de Toros México
The largest bull ring in the Western Hemisphere, it seats more than 40,000 spectators. The top matadors perform on Sunday afternoons from November through February. ◎ Augusto Rodin 241 • 5611-4413 • www.lamexico.com

Estadio Azul
The 39,000-seat stadium is home to one of Mexico City's most popular soccer clubs, Cementeros de Cruz Azul. ◎ Insurgentes Sur at Holbein, Col Nápoles • www.cruz-azul.com.mx

Parque Hundido
This park, with flower gardens, fountains, pine trees, and walking paths lined with replicas of pre-Hispanic sculpture, is a neighborhood favorite *(see p47)*.

Universidad Nacional Autónoma de México
Latin America's largest university is also known for its modern architecture and exceptional murals on the facades of several buildings *(see p45)*.

Price Categories

For a three course meal for one with half a bottle of wine (or equivalent meal), taxes, and extra charges.

$	under 150 pesos
$$	150–250 pesos
$$$	250–350 pesos
$$$$	350–450 pesos
$$$$$	over 450 pesos

Left **Metro Toro** Right **Rosetta**

🔟 Places to Eat

1 Mero Toro
Mexican politicians and actors flock to this attractive restaurant specializing in seafood. ⓢ *Amsterdam 204, Col Condesa • Map H5 • 5564-7799 • Closed Mon • $$$$$*

2 La Buena Tierra
This popular café offers many organic foods and fresh juices, plus creative fish, chicken, and vegetarian entrées. ⓢ *Atlixco 94 Col Condesa • Map G6 • 5211-4242 • www.labuenatierra.com • $$*

3 El Tizoncito
This simple restaurant claims to have invented *tacos al pastor* (kabob-style pork). Whether this is true or not, they serve the best in the city. ⓢ *Tamaulipas 122, near Nuevo León, Col Condesa • Map G6 • 5286-7321 • $$*

4 Don Asado
Fire-roasted Uruguayan meats and wood-fired pizzas are the specialty at this popular café. ⓢ *Michoacán 77, Col Condesa • Map G6 • 5286-0789 • www.donasado.com • $$*

5 Matisse
This cozy restaurant serves fine European cuisine. Try the baked chicken in blackberry sauce and duck à la blueberry. ⓢ *Amsterdam 260, Col Condesa • Map H5 • 5264-5853 • www.matisse.com.mx • $$$$*

6 Rosetta
The best Italian food in the city is served in this beautifully restored mansion. They also make excellent breads to take out. Reservations are essential. ⓢ *Colima 166, Col Roma • Map K5 • 5533-7804 • Closed Sun • $$$$$*

7 Tecla
Sample innovative appetizers such as squash flowers stuffed with goat cheese and served with *chipotle* sauce at this restaurant. Entrées include Roquefort steak and trout. ⓢ *Av Durango 186A, Col Roma • Map H4 • 5525-4920 • $$*

8 Contramar
Casual bright decor and fresh seafood prepared with a refined flourish make Contramar a highly popular choice. ⓢ *Durango 200, Col Roma • Map H4 • 5514-3169 • 1:30–6:30pm • Reservations recommended • $$$$*

9 Litoral
Litoral serves good Mexican cuisine such as crab tacos, onion soup, and salmon. ⓢ *55B Tamaulipas, Col Condesa • Map G5 • 5286-2015 • www.restaurantelitoral.com • $$$$*

10 Bistrot Mosaico
Try some of the excellent French food served at this bistro. ⓢ *Michoacán 10, Col Condesa • Map G5 • 5584-2932 • $$$*

STREETSMART

MEXICO CITY'S TOP 10

Left **Mexico City, a welcoming place for children** Right **Tourist information kiosk**

TOP 10 Planning Your Trip

1 Visitor Centers
Before arriving, check the website for the Secretariat of Tourism (Federal) and the Virtual Guide. After arrival, stop by one of the offices or kiosks of Departamento de Turismo del Distrito Federal for information.

2 Media
Current events and cultural programs are listed in the weekly *Tiempo Libre*. The biweekly *DF por Travesías* covers clubs, bars, and restaurants. The English daily *The Herald*, is also available in newsstands.

3 Internet
Many hotels offer Internet access either at a business center or in the hotel lobby while some also offer direct access from the rooms. Many tourist areas have Internet cafés.

4 Maps
The Visitor Centers distribute an excellent, free *Mexico City Tourist Map*. Both Spanish and English versions are available. *Guía Roji* also has good city maps.

5 Visas and Identification
Citizens of North America and many countries in Europe and Latin America do not need a visa. Tourist permits should be obtained at the border. Entry requirements are prone to change so check

before travel. A passport is the most reliable identification. Citizens returning to the US will need a valid passport or other accepted official ID.

6 Insurance
Obtain travel and medical insurance before arriving in Mexico. If you are entering Mexico by car, you must carry Mexican auto insurance.

7 When to Go
Mexico City is a year-round destination. March and early April are particularly beautiful.

8 What to Take
Conservative city-casual clothing is suitable for most occasions. Mexicans do not wear shorts though. Try to avoid carrying high-priced items.

9 How Long to Stay
A week is ideal, allowing three to four days to explore the Centro Histórico and the museums in Bosque de Chapultepec. Two days are best for exploring Coyoacán, San Ángel, and Xochimilco. Allow a full day for Teotihuacán.

10 Traveling with Children
Children must have proof of citizenship. If the child is traveling alone or with just one parent, carry notarized letters of permission from the absent parent.

Directory

Secretariat of Tourism (Federal) – SECTUR
Av Presidente Masarik 172, Col Polanco • *01-800-987-8224, 3002-6300* • *www. sectur.gob.mx*

Virtual Guides
www.mexicocity.com, www.mexicocity.gob. mx

Infotour
078 • *24-hour English language information*

Visitor Center Mexico City Airport, National Arrivals
5786-9002 • *www. mexicocity.gob.mx*

Visitor Center Zona Rosa
Paseo de la Reforma s/n, next to Angel de la Independencia

Visitor Center Centro Histórico
Next to the Catedral Metropolitana

Visitor Center Bellas Artes
Av Juárez and Angela Peralta

Visitor Center Bosque de Chapultepec
In front of the Museo Nacional de Antropología

Visitor Center Coyoacán
Casa Municipal, Plaza Hidalgo 1

Visitor Center Xochimilco
Nuevo Embarcadero

Aeropuerto Internacional Benito Juárez

🔟 Getting to Mexico City

By Air
Many North, Central, and South American as well as European airlines have flights to the city. ✪ *Aeropuerto Internacional Benito Juárez • 2482-2400 (Terminal 1), 2598-7000 (Terminal 2) • www.asa. gob.mx*

Arriving
Stop at immigration to fill out a form to obtain a Tourist Card. It can be valid for 60–180 days.

Tickets and Fares
Air fares vary greatly. Peak times, such as summer and Christmas, are the most expensive times to travel. Fixed-date returns are always cheaper than open returns.

Getting into the City
Travelers with luggage or on a tight schedule should take a prepaid airport taxi. There is a Metro stop at the airport, but luggage is not permitted onboard.

Metro
If you have little luggage, the Metro is an option. Follow the signs to station Terminal Aérea which is on Metro line 5. If you are heading downtown, take the train to the Pantitlán station and switch to line 1. Depending on your final destination you may need to switch lines again. Check the map at the terminal before boarding.

Taxi
If you are using a taxi, purchase your prepaid fare from a booth of the Transportación Terrestre. Rates are set by zone, and are for the taxi not per person. The yellow and white airport taxis are safer than regular taxis.

Driving into Mexico City
There are excellent highways leading into Mexico City. Mexico 15-D, 57-D, and 85-D are the main toll roads from the north and west. Mexico 95-D and 150-D enter from the south and east. These are the fastest and most direct routes, and the toll roads (signified by the D) have less traffic. In other roads, traffic is almost always very heavy.

Bus
Buses are the most popular way to travel between cities. First class buses have comfortable seats, videos, and make fewer stops. Boletotal has a central reservations system for major bus companies. ETN, with services to north-central Mexico, and UNO, with services to Oaxaca, Chiapas, Veracruz, and the southeast, are the luxury bus operators. Greyhound offers bus trips to major US cities. ✪ *Boletotal: 5133-5133, (01-800)-009-9090 • www.boletotal.mx* ✪ *ETN: 01-800-800-0386 • www. etn.com.mx* ✪ *UNO: 5133-5133, 01-800-737-5856; from the US: (01-800) 950-0287 • www.uno.com.mx* ✪ *Greyhound: 01-800-710-8819 • www.greyhound.com.mx*

Bus Terminals
There are four main bus terminals. Terminal Central de Autobuses del Norte (for northern destinations), Terminal Central de Autobuses Sur (south), Terminal de Autobuses de Pasajeros de Oriente (east), and Terminal de Autobuses del Poniente (west). ✪ *Terminal Central de Autobuses del Norte: Av Cien Metros 4907 • 5587-1552 • www.central delnorte.com.mx* ✪ *Terminal Central de Autobuses Sur: Av Taxqueña 1320 • 5689-9745* ✪ *Terminal de Autobuses de Pasajeros de Oriente: Ignacio Zaragoza 200 • 5133-5133* ✪ *Terminal de Autobuses del Poniente: Río Tacubaya 232, Col Real del Monte • 5271-4519 • www. centralponiente.com.mx*

Rental Cars
The major rental car companies have booths at the airport. It is usually cheaper to book a car before arriving in Mexico. Driving in the city is not easy; consider hiring a car with a driver or using hotel and *sitio* taxis (licensed and regulated taxis). You must obey the *Hoy No Circula* law, introduced to curb pollution, which says that one day a week, based on the last digit of the vehicle license plate, the car cannot be driven in Greater Mexico City.

Left **Metro subway car** Right **Turibus**

Getting Around

1 Metro
The Metro subway system is clean, efficient, cheap, and easy to use *(see backflap)*. During rush hour it is extremely crowded. Some cars are then set aside for women and children. ⊗ *5am–midnight Mon–Sat, 6am–midnight Sun • 3 pesos per ride • www.metro.df.gob.mx*

2 Buses, Peseros, Metrobus
Mexico City has a vast, confusing, and poorly marked bus system that covers most of the city. Routes and numbers change frequently, there are buses of different sizes, and the signs on the buses are often incorrect. ⊗ *5am–10pm daily • About 5 pesos depending on the bus size and the distance traveled*

3 Taxi
There are three types of taxi services. Roving cabs are hailed on the street but these are not recommended. Taxis from a *sitio* stand are safer. Hotel taxis are the most reliable and the driver often speaks English. Some taxis are metered, and others charge a flat fare. ⊗ *Sitio Taxi Service: Servitaxi • 5516-6020, 5516-6025 ⊗ Sitio Taxi Service: Radio-Taxi • 5566-0077*

4 Car with Driver
A good, time-efficient option for seeing parts of the city not readily accessible by walking,

bus tours, or Turibus is to hire a car and driver by the hour. The price varies by the services provided, but drivers will wait while you explore and even accompany you into markets. ⊗ *About 100–350 pesos per hour*

5 Turibus
For a daily fee you can hop on and off the bus all day long at 21 stops, conveniently located close to the major attractions in Centro Histórico, along Paseo de la Reforma, through Bosque de Chapultepec, Polanco, Condesa, and Zona Rosa. There is also a Turibus South making 15 stops along Coyoacán, including Museo Frida Kahlo and World Trade Center. ⊗ *5133-2488 • 9am–9pm daily (Zócalo, Chapultepec, Polanco) • www.turibus.com.mx*

6 Turibus Villa de Guadalupe/ Basílica de Guadalupe and Teotihuacán
These Turibus trips include admission, guided tours, and a buffet as well as transportation. ⊗ *5133-2488 • 9am daily from Auditorio Nacional and Zócalo • Adult 700 pesos, children (under 11) 450 pesos*

7 Trolleybus
The trolleybus offers narrated tours in Spanish, and provides a good introduction to the major sites. ⊗ *Tranvía Turístico*

Cultural: Av Juárez 66 • 5542-0083 • 10am–5pm daily • 30 pesos ⊗ Paseo por Coyoacán: Av Hidalgo at Allende • 5658-4027 • 11am–6pm daily • 45 pesos

8 Walking
Walking, during the day, is a great way to explore the city. In Centro Histórico it is quicker to walk between sites. The monuments along Paseo de la Reforma are best viewed by walking its length. Coyoacán, San Ángel, Polanco, and Bosque de Chapultepec are all great for walking. Take care while crossing roads.

9 Tours
Many hotels have affiliated travel agencies that arrange tours to the most popular sites and usually feature bilingual guides. Nightlife tours typically include dinner, a show, and stop at Plaza Garibaldi. Sunday tours to bullfights are also organized *(see pp62–3)*. ⊗ *Hotel Imperial Travel Agency: Hotel Imperial, Paseo de la Reforma 64 • 5705-4911 • www.hotel imperial.com.mx*

10 Car
Mexico City's poorly marked maze of one-way streets makes navigation tricky. The *Hoy No Circula* law, introduced to curb vehicular pollution, is strictly enforced. ⊗ *www.mexicocity.com. mx/nocircula.html*

Pay for Metro and bus tickets with loose pocket change and avoid showing a wallet or cash

Left **Tourists wearing hats in the sun** Center **Traffic snarls** Right **Street food stall**

🔟 Things to Avoid

1 Driving in Mexico City
Avoid driving anywhere in greater Mexico City during rush hours. Also, never leave any of your valuables in a parked car.

2 Street Crime
Pickpockets and purse or camera snatching are the most common threats and can occur anywhere. Avoid wearing expensive jewelry and leave your valuables in a hotel safe. Stick to the main tourist streets when walking, and avoid walking at night. Use hotel or *sitio* taxis for evening transportation.

3 Street Taxi
Never use a street taxi for transportation. Rather use hotel or *sitio* taxis. A high proportion of violent crimes against tourists results from using roving taxis.

4 Food and Water
The tap water in Mexico City should not be consumed. Some of the high-quality hotels have their own water-filtration systems. Many higher-priced restaurants use filtered or bottled water. In casual or lower-priced restaurants only drink bottled beverages without ice. Avoid street food in general, but in particular food that is not freshly cooked and served hot, or that uses uncooked greens such as lettuce and cilantro (coriander).

5 Turista
Some travelers take a few days to adjust to the local foods and may get *turista*. Nausea, diarrhea, stomach cramps, and a light fever are the symptoms. If it occurs, drink plenty of bottled water, and eat bland, well-cooked food for a while. Symptoms should disappear within a few days. But if not, consult a doctor. In the initial days after arriving in Mexico City it helps to eat moderately and avoid highly spiced and unfamiliar foods.

6 Sunburn and Dehydration
The sun is intense in the high altitudes of Mexico City, and it is a good idea to apply sunscreen and wear a broad brimmed sunhat for protection. Wear sunglasses for your eyes. Dehydration is a common problem, and it is important to carry bottled water with you and drink liquids regularly.

7 Altitude Sickness
Mexico City is at 7,350 ft (2,240 m) above sea level, and if you are arriving from a much lower altitude, you should allow a few days before engaging in strenuous activity. If you have symptoms such as headaches or shortness of breath, it helps to drink plenty of water and be moderate in the use of coffee, tea, and alcohol.

8 Pollution
Air pollution can pose a health risk in Mexico City, especially for the elderly, young children, and people with heart or respiratory problems. The city is located in a large valley surrounded by high mountains with thermal inversions, which often trap pollutants. Smoking is prohibited in indoor public places, but there are some exceptions. Fines are steep so check before lighting up.

9 Watch Your Step
Mexico City was built on an old lake bed, and everywhere you go you will see buildings that have sunk below street level, and many that are tilting as well. The city has also experienced severe earthquakes, which have left uneven streets and sidewalks in many places. Watch your step while you walk.

10 Weather and Temperature Changes
Most tourists will notice minor weather changes, with cool mornings and nights that require a jacket. Rain storms can occur in the afternoon at any time of the year, and an umbrella or rain jacket will be useful. In winters make sure either your hotel is heated or that it provides extra blankets. In summers you will want either an air conditioned room or a good fan.

Rush hour in Mexico City is from about 8–10am and 3–7pm on weekdays

Left **Band playing live at the Zócalo** Right **Guide explaining architecture to tourists**

TOP10 Budget Tips

1 Airline Deals
The best prices are obtained by comparison shopping, and the Internet is a great source for checking ticket prices. If you are flying within the country after your arrival in Mexico City, check Mexican airlines for reduced rate advance purchase coupons, but you must purchase them before arriving in Mexico.

2 Package Deals
When shopping for the best airfares, check the websites for packages that include accommodations as well. Rates will likely be higher during Christmas, Easter, and the summer months. Some hotels offer deals that include city tours or tickets to events.

3 Hotel Discounts
Room rates fluctuate depending on time of year and if festivals or conventions are being held. Business hotels in Mexico City often offer good rates for weekends, and some hotels in Centro Histórico offer discounts as well. Mid-range and budget hotels may offer discounts for cash payments.

4 Free Museum Day
Many museums offer free admission either on Sunday or Tuesday, and for Mexican citizens and residents. Special discounts are sometimes available for students and teachers with ID.

5 Entertainment and Attractions
Several of Mexico City's top attractions are free, including the Palacio Nacional *(see pp16–17)*, Catedral Metropolitana *(see pp14–15)*, and a few of the attractions in Bosque de Chapultepec *(see pp24–5)*. All of the churches, parks, and plazas have free entry.

6 Tours and Guides
Hiring a guide or joining a tour that includes transportation will often save a lot of time and trouble, and sometimes money as well, especially if you are not fluent in Spanish.

7 Public Transportation
Sitio taxis are reasonably safe and are also cheaper than hotel taxis. The Turibus *(see p104)* is less expensive than cabs if you are visiting sites it covers. The Metro *(see p104)* also offers cheap, efficient, and quite an extensive service.

8 Free Events
Every Sunday evening Mexico City's Cultural Institute presents free concerts of Mexican talent at the Zócalo. For information on other such events see *Tiempo Libre (see p102)* and check the mexicocity website.

9 Restaurants
Save money by having lunch, from 2pm until 4pm, at one of the many restaurants serving a *comida corrida* (fixed-priced menu).

10 Location
When choosing a hotel consider the transportation method you plan to use within the city to reduce your traveling costs.

Directory

Airlines
• Aeroméxico:
5133-4000;
www.aeromexico.com

• Air Canada:
www.aircanada.com

• Air France:
www.airfrance.com

• American Airlines:
www.aa.com

• British Airways:
www.britishairways.com

• United:
www.united.com

Travel Websites
• www.airline
consolidator.com

Best Fares
• www.bestfares.com

Cheap Tickets
• www.cheap
tickets.com
• www.exitotravel.com
• www.expedia.com
• www.hotwire.com
• www.orbitz.com
• www.priceline.com
• www.travelocity.com

Free Events
• www.mexicocity.
gob.mx

Left **Spanish-English dictionaries** Right **Tourist taking a photograph of a *mariachi***

TOP 10 Etiquette

1 Courtesy
Courtesy is important in Mexico City, and even a simple, *buenos días* (good morning), or *buenas tardes* (good afternoon), is much appreciated. The Mexican communication style is lengthy and indirect; losing your temper or complaining about a situation often makes people less inclined to help you out.

2 Friendly and Helpful
Mexicans are friendly and helpful, especially if you make an attempt to ask questions in Spanish. However, they also do not like to say "no," so they will often respond to a question by giving an answer even if they are not certain. When seeking directions, ask several people. Most employees take their own job responsibilities seriously and will seldom bend the rules or make any exceptions.

3 Language
Many Mexicans speak a few words of English, especially college and high school students, but it helps to know some basic phrases for use at restaurants, with *sitio* taxis, and getting around. Pick up some useful Spanish phrases *(see pp126–7)* and carry a handy Spanish-English dictionary.

4 Service
Many Mexicans will offer a personal service in exchange for a small fee, and there are times when you may want to utilize these services. Hotel and *sitio* taxi drivers can accompany you into markets if you ask them to, wait while you visit an attraction, or pick you up at a specified time – all for a reasonable charge.

5 Attire
In Mexico City people dress conservatively; they wear very little jewelry, and do not wear shorts or sandals. They are tolerant of other styles of attire; however, women traveling alone will do well to dress conservatively when out in public to avoid unwanted attention.

6 Single Women
Mexican *machismo* is very common in the city, and can be both a benefit and a hassle for the single woman traveling alone. On the plus side, men will assist you if you are in difficulty and male tour guides may pay you more attention. You can minimize advances by dressing conservatively and avoiding eye contact. However, if you are still approached a simple "no" and a shake of the head is often enough. Taking a seat will lessen the risk of unwanted attention on a crowded Metro.

7 Public Toilets
Public toilets are not common in the city, but most sit-down restaurants have clean bathrooms for their customers. Many public bathrooms have an attendant and you pay a few pesos to enter; be certain to take the toilet paper they hand out.

8 Time
Mexico City is in the Central Standard Time Zone, which is 6 hours behind Greenwich Mean Time. Although Mexico City has a reputation for not being punctual, most people in tourism and in business are prompt with appointments.

9 Tipping
A tip of 10 percent is standard in restaurants, but check your bill first as some restaurants add a service charge to the total. For porters and bellhops, 10 pesos per bag is enough. Taxi drivers are tipped if they provide a special service. For tour guides, a tip of 50 or more pesos for four hours is usual.

10 Photography
Mexicans are generally tolerant towards photographers taking pictures, but it is always polite to ask first. Some people will request a small payment, and many indigenous people will refuse to have their picture taken.

Left **Mexican Tourist Police** Center **Hospital** Right **Logo of a pharmacy store chain**

🔟 Security and Health

1 Embassies and Consulates
International visitors who lose a passport or have any similar emergency, should contact their embassy immediately.

2 Keeping Documents Safe
Before leaving home, make photocopies of all your important travel papers, including your passport and visa, as well as the numbers of credit cards and the serial numbers of travelers' checks. Keep them in a safe place in your hotel.

3 Crime
Mexico City has a relatively high level of street crime, and it is important to be vigilant at all times. It is best to use ATM machines in safe locations during the day. Leave surplus valuables in the hotel safe. Walk around the city on foot only in daylight hours. Stick to the streets frequented by tourists.

4 Emergencies
In the case of an emergency it is probably best to try and contact your embassy first. The Mexico City Tourist Protection Agency will also help with emergencies and they have staff who speak English. If you cannot reach an English speaking operator, call the SECTUR 24-hour Hotline for help.

5 Police
When approached by the police be polite, remain calm, and explain that you are a tourist. If a policeman asks for a bribe call your embassy immediately.

6 Stay Alert
Mexico City does have crime; however, if you stay alert and take some simple precautions you should be fine. Stay on the main tourist streets when walking, dress conservatively, and avoid carrying or wearing anything that appears to be valuable. Be cautious while using an ATM.

7 Safety
Be especially careful at night, and for transport use a hotel taxi or *sitio* taxi rather than walking or using any other means of public transportation.

8 Public Restrooms
Public restrooms, referred to as *baños* or *sanitarios*, which are clean and hygienic can be found in mid- to large-size restaurants, the lobby area of large hotels, and in major museums and tourist attractions.

9 Medical Care
For basic medical and dental needs, ask your hotel or embassy for help. One of the best hospitals in Mexico City is the Hospital ABC, with staff speaking in English.

10 Pharmacies
The largest and most commonly found pharmacies in Mexico City are Farmacias del Ahorro and Fenix.

Directory

Embassies
• Australia: 1101-2200, www.mexico.embassy.gov.au
• Canada: 5724-7900, www.canada.org.mx
• USA: 5080-2000, www.usembassy-mexico.gov
• Britain: 1670-3200, http://ukinmexico.fco.gov.uk

Banks
• BBVA Bancomer: 5226-2663
• Banamex: 1226-2639

Lost Cards and Travelers' Checks
• American Express: 01800 001 3600
• MasterCard: 5480-8000, 001 800 307 7309
• Visa: 001 800 847 2911

Emergencies
• Tourist Protection Agency (SECTUR): 078
• Ambulance: 065
• Police: 060
• Missing person or car: 5658-1111

Medical Care
• Hospital ABC: 5230-8000; 5230-8161 (emergencies)
• Mexican Red Cross: 5395-1111

Pharmacies
www.fahorro.com.mx

 Notify your credit card companies of your travel dates and ask them for telephone numbers that work from Mexico

Left **A courier office** Center **Mexican phone card** Right **Telmex logo**

🔟 Banking and Communications

1 Exchange
The airport is a good place to exchange foreign currency for pesos. The exchange rate at a *Casa de Cambio* (foreign exchange booths) may be better or worse than what the major branches of large banks offer.

2 ATMs
ATM machines are readily available throughout the city, and are usually available 24 hours a day and seven days a week. However, it is always a good idea to withdraw money during daylight hours and at an off-street machine in a bank or department store for reasons of safety.

3 Banks
Banamex and BBVA Bancomer are the two largest banks in Mexico. There are also numerous foreign banks in the city. Hours are generally 9am–4pm weekdays, and many banks are open on Saturdays from 9am–2pm. It is best to visit a bank in the morning as some services, including currency exchange, are only available until 2pm.

4 Travelers' Checks
Although travelers' checks are one of the safest ways to carry cash, very few places in Mexico City accept them. American Express travelers' checks in US currency are the best choice, and most large banks and currency exchange offices will cash them. 🔾 *American Express: Paseo de la Reforma 350A, at Lancaster • 01800 504 0400 • 9am–6pm Mon–Fri, 9am–1pm Sat*

5 Credit Cards
Visa and MasterCard, and to a lesser extent American Express, are the most accepted cards in Mexico. Most high-end restaurants, large hotels, rental cars, and high-end tourist shops will accept credit cards. Some hotels offer discounts for cash, while others will add a surcharge to the amount if paid by credit card.

6 Telephone
The country code for Mexico is 52, and the area code for Mexico City is 55. Within the city the important dialing codes are 040 for information and 090 for an international English speaking operator.

7 Phone Cards
Most payphones in Mexico City require a prepaid phone card, known as a Ladatel Card, issued by the main telephone company, Telmex. Available in denominations of 30, 50, and 100 pesos, they can be purchased at newsstands, pharmacies, and grocery stores. The phones are generally very easy to find along the street as well as in gas and Metro stations.

8 Internet
Public access to the Internet is quite easy to find, and is available in the lobby or in the business center of many hotels. Ask at the front desk for the nearest location. Some hotels provide wireless networks, while others offer data access lines. Always learn the rates before using the services. Internet cafés can be found throughout the city and generally charge about 25 pesos an hour.

9 Post Office
The Mexican post office can be slow with the delivery of mail or packages. It is much safer and more reliable to use a courier service. Many hotels sell stamps for letters and post cards, and will also post them.

🔟 Courier Services
For shipping important documents and parcels a courier service is the best option to use. There are several to choose from, including Federal Express, DHL, Estafeta, AeroMexpress, and United Parcel Service (UPS). They will pick-up packages from your premises with 24 hours' advance notice. 🔾 *Federal Express: www.fedex.com* 🔾 *DHL: www.dhl.com* 🔾 *Estafeta: www.estafeta.com* 🔾 *AeroMexpress: www.aeromexpress.com.mx* 🔾 *UPS: www.ups.com*

Left **Mexican handicrafts on display** Right **A Mexico City market**

TOP 10 Shopping Tips

1 Shopping Hours
Department stores and shopping malls are generally open from 10am–7pm Monday through Saturday. Art galleries are generally open on Sundays, but closed on Mondays and some of them require advance appointments. Boutique stores usually open at 10am, but may close from about 1pm to 3pm, and then reopen.

2 Paying and Bargaining
High-end storefronts, department stores, and most boutiques do not entertain bargaining. But bargaining certainly is part of the experience of shopping in the *mercados*, or markets. How much to bargain for varies by market and by vendor. The best is to simply decide what the item is worth to you, and bargain accordingly.

3 Mercados
Mercados, or markets, are the traditional shopping venues for Mexicans, and they are still the most fascinating places to shop. Most neighborhoods have one or more *mercados*. Even if you are not shopping for anything, walking through a market is an excellent cultural experience.

4 Boutiques
During the day, Zona Rosa, with its many clothing boutiques, is one of the most popular shopping districts in the city, especially with tourists. The chic, high-end fashion boutiques are primarily located along Avenida Presidente Masarik in Polanco and also along Altavista Street in San Ángel.

5 Art Galleries
Art galleries are found in many parts of Mexico City. Polanco is best known for its high-end galleries and design studios, while Zona Rosa offers a mix of fine art galleries and antique shops which also offer a huge variety of art.
Ⓢ www.arte-mexico.com

6 Department Stores and Shopping Malls
There are two major department store chains in Mexico City – El Palacio de Hierro, an upscale department store chain, that specializes in designer clothing, and Liverpool which offers a wide range of mid-priced products and clothing. Antara Polanco is a fashionable shopping center. Centro Santa Fe, with more than 300 stores, is the largest shopping center in Mexico. Ⓢ *El Palacio de Hierro: www.palaciode hierro.com.mx* Ⓢ *Liverpool: www.liverpool.com.mx* Ⓢ *Antara Polanco: Av Moliére and Av Ejército Nacional, Col Polanco* Ⓢ *Centro Santa Fe: Av Vasco de Quiroga*

7 Museum Stores
Mexico City's museums offer some of the most interesting shops in the city. The merchandise reflects the museums' collections, and selections vary from CDs and books about performing arts at the Palacio de Bellas Artes *(see pp22–3)*, to prints of Frida Kahlo's famous works at Museo Frida Kahlo *(see p89)*.

8 Souvenirs
One of the best places to shop for Mexican handicrafts and souvenirs is at Mercado de Artesanías de la Ciudadela *(see p53)*. Across from the Zócalo, along Monte de Piedad, many fine silver shops offer jewelry in a range of tempting prices.

9 Mexican Crafts
Mexican handicrafts can be found at Fonart *(see p78)*, Museo de Artes Popular *(see p70)*, Arte Mexicano para el Mundo *(see p72)*, and Mercado de Artesanías de la Ciudadela *(see p53)*. Víctor Artes Populares is for the serious collector. Ⓢ *Víctor Artes Populares, 3rd floor, Av Madero 10* • 5512-1263 • *12:30–7pm Mon–Fri*

10 Religious Art
The gift shop at the Villa de Guadalupe *(see pp30–31)* is a great place to find a huge collection of religious art.

Left **Many hotels have in-house tour agencies** Right *Comida*

Eating and Accommodation Tips

Restaurant Types

Mexican street food is found near every Metro station, in the markets, and on busy street corners. The small restaurants known as *taquerías* offer the same type of food as the street vendors, but generally with higher hygienic standards. *Fondas* are small cafés that offer *comida*, a fixed-menu lunch. Cantinas are popular in the evening as they serve food as well as liquor. Restaurants come in all sizes and price ranges, from modest cafés to chic five-star restaurants.

Breakfast

Desayuno (breakfast), is traditionally a large meal of *huevos* (eggs), served in a variety of ways. Most egg dishes come with a heavy spicy red or green sauce (salsa) and are usually served with refried beans and hot tortillas. *Chorizo* is a popular sausage. Lighter breakfasts feature *pan dulce*, a sweet bread, or *bolillos*, which is a European-style roll.

Lunch

Comida, or lunch, is the large meal of the day. Lunch is a relaxed affair with friends, and can often last for hours. Many restaurants offer a daily *comida corrida* special, often featuring several courses and at an excellent price.

Dinner

Traditionally dinner was a very light meal of a sweet bread and hot chocolate. *Churros*, fried dough pastry coated with sugar, and hot chocolate remain a favorite evening snack. Many Mexicans now have a large evening meal and plenty of restaurants offer full dinner menus.

Tipping and Taxes

In restaurants it is traditional to tip 10–15 percent of the total amount, but some places include the tip in the total. A value added tax of 15 percent is added to services, goods, and hotels. In addition, hotels add a further 2 percent accommodations tax.

Hotel Taxis

Hotel taxis are the easiest and most convenient-to-use taxi service. They can be hired by the trip, by the hour, or for all day. The drivers associated with high-end hotels speak English and Spanish, are sometimes certified tourist guides, and can take you on personalized tours of your choice of city attractions. Negotiate the rates before boarding the taxi.

Hotel Tours

Hotel tours can be a fun way to see the city and meet other travelers, and they alleviate a lot of the transportation hassles and logistics issues. On the other hand, you are sometimes rushed around sights. Make sure that the guide speaks your language.

Hotel Fitness Facilities

If exercising is important for you, make sure you understand what facilities the hotel has when you make your reservations. Many of the high-end hotels either have their own facilities or can make arrangements for you to use other facilities close to the hotel.

Getting the Best Rate

Hotel rates are often negotiable, especially if you are flexible regarding your dates of stay. Many business hotels are busy during the week, but offer great discounts for weekend stays. Some hotels will give discounts if you pay in cash.

Camping

There are two campgrounds located just outside Greater Mexico City. Both have facilities for RVs and tents. Pepe's *(see p117)* in Tepotzotlán, to the northwest of the city, offers camping in an in-town walled hacienda-like campground. To the north of the city is Teotihuacán Trailer Park offering camping facilities. Ⓢ *Teotihuacán Trailer Park, Adolfo López Mateos 17, San Juan Teotihuacán* • *(594) 956-0313*

Left **María Isabel Sheraton** Center **Hotel Gran Meliá** Right **Staircase, Embassy Suites**

🔟 Luxury Hotels

1 Hotel Four Seasons

This modern Neo-Classical hotel is renowned for its service and modern comfort. Another advantage of staying here is the Four Seasons' close proximity to the Museo Nacional de Antropología. The hotel has a breathtaking eight-story central courtyard garden and fountain. ✪ *Paseo de la Reforma 500, Col Juárez • Map G3 • 5230-1818 • www.fourseasons.com/mexico • $$$$$*

2 St Regis

This high-rise hotel is the most luxurious in town, attracting high caliber guests such as Placido Domingo and Lady Gaga. The St Regis also boasts great spa facilities, and you can even land your helicopter on the roof.✪ *Paseo de la Reforma 439, Col Cuauhtémoc • Map G3 • 5228-1818 • www.starwoodhotels.com • $$$$$*

3 María Isabel Sheraton

This is a classic high-rise hotel with an expansive marble lobby, friendly service, and an excellent location directly across from the Monumento a la Independencia with its golden angel. ✪ *Paseo de la Reforma 325, Col Cuauhtémoc • Map J4 • 5242-5555 • www.starwoodhotels.com • $$$$$*

4 Marquis Reforma

Subtle and serene, this low-rise pink granite and glass luxury hotel is done up in Art Deco style and offers excellent service. It is located between Zona Rosa and Bosque de Chapultepec. ✪ *Paseo de la Reforma 465, Col Cuauhtémoc • Map N5 • 5229-1234 • www.marquisreforma.com • $$$$$*

5 Fiesta Americana Reforma

In addition to spacious rooms and suites, business services, a fitness center, and a kids' club, this world-class hotel opposite the Glorieta de Colón offers two restaurants and a bar with live music every night. ✪ *Paseo de la Reforma 80, Col Juárez • Map L3 • 5140-4100 • www.fiestamericana.com • $$$$$*

6 W

The hotel has a contemporary design and the decor is tastefully elegant although accented in pulsating red. The hotel features the Away Spa and Fitness Center, and is within walking distance of Bosque de Chapultepec. ✪ *Campos Elíseos 252, Col Polanco • 9138-1800 • www.whotels.com/mexicocity • $$$$$*

7 Hotel Gran Meliá

Elegant and modern, this beautiful hotel with its 20-story atrium lobby has spacious guestrooms fitted with dark wood furnishings. ✪ *Paseo de la Reforma, 1 Mexico City • Map M2 • 5128-5000 • www.granmelia mexicoreforma.com • $$$*

8 JW Marriott

This sophisticated high-rise hotel has spacious guestrooms in European-style decor, warm colors, and high-speed Internet. Located close to Bosque de Chapultepec. ✪ *Andrés Bello 29, Col Polanco • Map C3 • 5999-0000 • www.marriott.com.mx • $$$$$*

9 Presidente InterContinental

This 42-story high-rise overlooks Bosque de Chapultepec in trendy Polanco. Excellent restaurants offer a choice of New York steakhouse, fine Mexican cuisine, great Italian food, or casual French bistro dining. ✪ *Campos Elíseos 218, Col Polanco • Map K4 • 5327-7700 • www.intercontinental.com • $$$$$*

10 Embassy Suites

This glass-fronted high-rise hotel on Paseo de la Reforma offers tasteful design, excellent service, and exceptional amenities, including a pool and a fitness center. ✪ *Paseo de la Reforma 69 • Map N1 • 5061-3000 • www.embassysuites.com • $$$*

Gran Hotel de la Ciudad de México

Price Categories		
For a standard, double room per night (with breakfast if included), taxes, and extra charges.	$	under 1000 pesos
	$$	1000–1500 pesos
	$$$	1500–2000 pesos
	$$$$	2000–2500 pesos
	$$$$$	over 2500 pesos

🏅10 Historic Hotels

1 Gran Hotel de la Ciudad de México

This 19th-century hotel, fronting the Zócalo, features a magnificent Art Nouveau lobby with a beautiful 1908 Tiffany stained-glass ceiling. It has an open courtyard, with a lovely, panoramic view from the elegant wrought-iron elevators. ✆ *Av 16 de Septiembre 82, Col Centro • Map P3 • 1083-7700 • www. granhotelciudaddemexico. com.mx • $$$$*

2 Hotel Majestic

The hotel is housed in a lovely Baroque building that fronts on the Zócalo. The lobby of the hotel features a red-tiled floor, lovely fountain, and hand-painted tiles from Pueblo. The rooftop Terraza Restaurant is an excellent place to watch the flag ceremony on the Zócalo. ✆ *Madero 73, Col Centro • Map Q3 • 5521-8600 • www.hotel majestic.com.mx • Not all rooms have air conditioning • $$*

3 Boutique Hotel de Cortés

This imposing former convent near the Centro Histórico dates from the 17th century but has been given a thoroughly modern facelift. The trendy rooftop bar overlooks the Alameda. ✆ *Av Hidalgo 85, Col Centro • Map N2 • 5518-2181 • www.boutiquehotelde cortes.com • $$$*

4 Imperial Hotel

This triangular five-story building was constructed in 1904, and when it opened it was the tallest building in Mexico City. The lobby has an elegant marble floor, a crystal chandelier suspended from the ceiling, and a sweeping grand stairway. ✆ *Paseo de la Reforma 64, Col Juárez • Map L3 • 5705-4911 • www. hotelimperial.com.mx • $$$*

5 Holiday Inn Zócalo

This historic colonial building located across from the Zócalo houses a thoroughly modern Holiday Inn with a glass front lobby. Comfortable guestrooms are decorated in a pleasant colonial style. ✆ *Av 5 de Mayo 61, Col Centro • Map Q2 • 5130-5130, 1-877-660-8550 • www.hotelescortes. com • $$*

6 Geneve Calinda

This elegant 1906 colonial hotel with classical European styling is decorated with antique furnishings and fine art. The attached Sanborns Restaurant is in a historic salon with stained-glass decor. ✆ *Londres 130, Col Juárez • Map H3 • 5080-0800 • www.hotelgeneve. com.mx • $$*

7 Hotel Ritz

Built in 1930 on one of the city's most historic streets, Madero, the hotel's rooms are smallish but clean and inviting. There is Internet available in the lobby and the staff are very friendly and helpful. ✆ *Madero 30, Col Centro • Map P2 • 5130-0169 • www. hotelritz.mx • No air conditioning • $$*

8 Hotel Gillow

Pleasant small hotel with a lovely century-old marble, brass, and dark-wood lobby. The sixth-floor rooms have private balconies. ✆ *Isabel la Católica 17, Col Centro • Map P2 • 5518-1440 • www.hotelgillow.com • No air conditioning • $$*

9 Hotel María Cristina

A small hotel in a charming rose-colored four-story colonial building close to the UK Embassy. The garden offers a retreat from the bustle of the city. ✆ *Río Lerma 31, Col Cuauhtémoc • Map J3 • 5703-1212 • www.hotelmariacristina. com.mx • Air conditioning only in some rooms • $$*

10 Hotel Catedral

This small hotel with 116 rooms has a lovely lobby with gleaming marble floors, dark woodwork, and arched windows. Two terraces on the seventh floor, with chairs and tables, provide great views of the city. ✆ *Donceles 95, Col Centro • Map Q2 • 5518-5232 • www.hotelcatedral.com • No air conditioning • $$*

Left **Hotel Brick** Right **Hotel Hábita**

TOP 10 Boutique Hotels and Inns

1 Casa González
This charming, colonial-style small inn, with 22 guestrooms and a lovely landscaped courtyard, is located in a residential area near the UK and US embassies. Each room is unique, and some have their own balcony or terrace. ❂ *Río Sena 69, Col Cuauhtémoc • Map J3 • 5514-3302 • www.hotelcasagonzalez. com • No air conditioning • $*

2 Hotel Hábita
Located in trendy Polanco, the ultra-modern design makes this 36-room boutique hotel a standout. Guestrooms offer an elegantly minimalist white and metal decor, marble baths, and comfortable beds. ❂ *Av Presidente Masarik 201, Col Polanco • Map D2 • 5282-3100 • www.hotelhabita.com • $$$$$*

3 Casa Vieja
This luxurious all-suites boutique hotel is housed in a 19th-century mansion in an exclusive section of Polanco. The two-story hacienda is elegantly charming, with tiled courtyard and common areas, colored stucco walls, and lavishly decorated with Mexican ceramics, paintings, and folk art. The suites are spacious with colorful decor. ❂ *Eugenio Sue 45, Col Polanco • Map D2 • 5282-0067 • www. casavieja.com • $$$$$*

4 Room Mate Valentina
This hotel in the heart of the Zona Rosa features colorful modern decor. Guests can enjoy a daily breakfast buffet and free Wi-Fi. There is also disabled access. ❂ *Amberes 27, Col Juárez • Map H3 • 5080-4500 • www.room-matehotels. com • $$*

5 The Red Tree House
The owners of this hotel treat their guests as if they were part of the family. Located in a leafy residential neighborhood, this place fills up fast, so it is wise to book well in advance. ❂ *Culiacan 6, Col Condesa • Map H6 • 5584-3829 • http://red tree.mexicoqt.com • $$$*

6 NH Centro Histórico
This is a small five-story boutique hotel with minimalist decor and pleasant common areas. The rooms are small and comfortable with wood floors. Many rooms offer city views and there is a rooftop restaurant. ❂ *Calle Palma 42, Centro • Map Q2 • 5130-1850 • www.nh-hotels.com • $$*

7 Hotel Emporium
This elegant boutique hotel presents European charm in a stunning early 20th-century building. The lobby is finished in pink marble with large mirrors and brass detailing. All guestrooms are tastefully decorated with contemporary colors and have modern baths with Jacuzzis. ❂ *Av Paseo de la Reforma 124, Col Juárez • Map L3 • 5566-7766 • www.hoteles emporio.com • $$$$*

8 Hotel Suites Amberes
Charming and modern, the suites of this small apartment-style boutique hotel feature full kitchens and a separate alcove. Guests are also served complimentary Mexican breakfast. ❂ *Amberes 64, Col Juárez • Map J4 • 5533-1306 • www.suitesamberes. com.mx • $$$$*

9 Las Alcobas
Designed by the renowned duo Yabu Pushelberg, this hotel in the heart of Polanco has an upscale vibe with an intimate tone. The excellent Dulce Patria restaurant *(see p87)* is just around the corner. ❂ *Av Presidente Masarik 390A, Col Polanco • 3300-3900 • www. lasalcobas.com • $$$$*

10 Hotel Brick
For chic, high-end design in trendy Colonia Roma, this remodeled former mansion is the place to stay. The terrace café/restaurant attracts a young and beautiful crowd. ❂ *Orizaba 95, Col Roma • Map K5 • 5525-1100 • www. hotelbrick.com • $$$$$*

Most hotels accept credit cards, but some mid-range and budget hotels expect cash

Price Categories

For a standard, double room per night (with breakfast if included), taxes, and extra charges.	**$**	under 1000 pesos
	$$	1000–1500 pesos
	$$$	1500–2000 pesos
	$$$$	2000–2500 pesos
	$$$$$	over 2500 pesos

Left **Plaza Florencia** Right **Royal Hotel Zona Rosa**

ᵀᴼᴾ10 Mid-Range Hotels

Galería Plaza
Located in Zona Rosa this 11-story hotel is a favorite with business travelers. The spacious and bright guestrooms are done up in a modern style using neutral colors. ⊗ *Hamburgo 195 Col Juárez • Map G3 • 5230-1717 • www.brisas.com.mx • $$$*

Sevilla Palace
This sleek 23-story high-rise hotel comes with modern rooms and a dramatic central atrium lobby with a welcoming sitting area. The excellent amenities include a fitness center, a rooftop pool, a hot tub, and a lounge. ⊗ *Av Paseo de la Reforma 105, Col Tabacalera • Map L3 • 5705-2800 • www. sevillapalace.com.mx • $$*

Hilton Centro Histórico Hotel and Convention Center
Conveniently located at the entrance to the historic center, the Hilton offers its guests a wide range of amenities, including wireless Internet access, fitness center, spa, relaxing pools, and even a private heliport, all in addition to top-class business facilities. The onsite restaurant El Cardenal offers superb Mexican and colonial cuisine. ⊗ *Av Juárez 70, Col Centro • Map N2 • 5130-5300 • www1.hilton.com • $$$*

Royal Hotel Zona Rosa
This small but classic Zona Rosa hotel has spacious rooms, with large baths. The rooms are tastefully decorated with neutral colors. The rooftop pool and solarium offer stunning views of the city. ⊗ *Amberes 78, Col Juárez • Map J4 • 9149-3000 • www. hotelroyalzr.com • $$$*

NH Mexico City
This contemporary Zona Rosa high-rise hotel has a sleek and modern lobby with marble floors and sitting areas. Large rooms are decorated in dark neutral colors with hardwood floors and matching wooden furniture. ⊗ *Liverpool 155, Col Juárez • Map H3 • 5228-9928 • www. nh-hotels.com • $$$*

Plaza Florencia
This narrow stone and glass tower in Zona Rosa has carpeted guestrooms with wood furnishings and neutral fabrics. ⊗ *Florencia 61, Col Juárez • Map H3 • 5242-4700 • www.plazaflorencia. com.mx • $$$*

Camino Real Polanco México
Located just off Paseo de la Reforma, this modern resort-hotel designed by Mexican architect Ricardo Legorreta has a collection of art works by Tamayo, Siqueiros, and others.

The hotel offers a modern gym, swimming pool, and sauna. ⊗ *Mariano Escobedo 700, Col Nueva Anzures • Map F2 • 5263-8888 • www.camino real.com • $$$$*

Century Hotel
Close to the gay nightlife section of Zona Rosa, this hotel offers comfortable guestrooms with private balconies, neutral color schemes, and marble baths with Roman tubs. The lovely lobby has marble floors, curved walls, and seating areas decorated in golden tones. ⊗ *Liverpool 152, Col Juárez • Map H3 • 5726-9911 • www. century.com.mx • $$$*

Fiesta Inn Centro Histórico
This is a modern hotel with 140 rooms furnished in neutral color tones. There is a small gym and a modern shopping mall on the first floor. ⊗ *Av Juárez 76, Col Centro • Map N2 • 5130-2900 • www.fiestainn.com • $$$*

Hotel Bristol
Situated in a quiet neighborhood behind the US and UK embassies, the hotel is a favorite with business and pleasure travelers. Attractive guestrooms, a convenient setting, and friendly staff make it a pleasant place to stay. ⊗ *Plaza Necaxa 17, Col Cuauhtémoc • Map K3 • 5533-6060 • www.hotel bristol.com.mx • $*

⇨ *Unless otherwise stated, all hotels have en-suite bathrooms and air conditioning*

Left **Foyer, Mexico City Hostel** Right **Hotel Palace**

Budget Hotels

1 Hotel Palace
This conveniently located hotel offers friendly service, tours to popular attractions, clean guestrooms decorated in blue tones, and an onsite restaurant. The Turibus stop is close by and the hotel is situated between Paseo de la Reforma and the Monumento a la Revolución. 🕲 *Ignacio Ramírez 7, Col Tabacalera • Map L2 • 5566-2400 • No air conditioning • $*

2 Mexico City Hostel
This cheery hostel in an attractive colonial building has a bilingual staff, Internet service, and a small café in the pretty lobby. Dormitory and private rooms are available, as are laundry services and lockers. 🕲 *República de Brasil 8, Col Centro • Map Q1 • 5512-3666 • www. mexicocityhostel.com • No air conditioning or private bathrooms • $*

3 Hostal Moneda
This hostel, just east of Zócalo, is popular with backpackers and includes airport pickup, breakfast buffet, Internet, and a pleasant rooftop terrace with hammocks. A basic room features bunk and in-room locker. 🕲 *Moneda 8, Col Centro • Map Q2 • 5522-5803 • www. hostalmoneda.com.mx • Air conditioning and private bathrooms only in some rooms • $*

4 Casa de los Amigos
This simple Quaker-run guest house caters to travelers who share their values of international peace and understanding. The place has shared dormitory-style rooms for men and women and a few small double rooms, with a minimum stay of four nights. 🕲 *Ignacio Mariscal 132, Col Tabacalera • Map L2 • 5705-0521 • www.casadelosamigos. org • Air conditioning and private bathrooms only in some rooms • $*

5 Hostel Mundo Joven Catedral
Affiliated to Hostelling International, this hostel has an attractive lobby with a full service café, friendly bilingual staff, and offers tours. Internet café, lockers, a roof-top terrace, and a complimentary breakfast are attractions. 🕲 *República de Guatemala 4, Col Centro • Map R2 • 5518-1726 • www. hostelcatedral.com • No air conditioning. Private bathrooms only in some rooms • $*

6 Hotel Isabel
Surrounding a large colonial courtyard, rooms at the Isabel are simple, spacious, and clean, with an old-fashioned, slightly faded vibe. Located near the Zócalo and Centro Histórico attractions. 🕲 *Isabel la Católica 63 • Map P3 • 5518-1213 • www. hotel-isabel.com.mx • $*

7 Posada Viena
This Mexican-style hotel has cozy rooms with large windows and ceiling fans. It also features an Argentine restaurant and wireless Internet in the public areas. 🕲 *Marsella 28, Col Juárez • Map K4 • 5592-7312 • www. posadavienahotel.com • Fourth night free. No air conditioning • $*

8 Hostal Centro Histórico Regina
This "retro art-kitsch youth hostel" is located in an area full of bars and restaurants. The rooftop terrace is a favorite hangout for backpackers. 🕲 *5 de Febrero 53 • Map Q4 • 5709-4192 • www. hostalcentrohistoricoregina. com • $*

9 Hostal Virreyes
On the edge of the Centro Histórico, this simple hostel has shared and private rooms, and offers good long-term rates. The lobby attracts an arty crowd for exhibitions and concerts. 🕲 *Izazága 8, Col Centro • Map P4 • 5521-4180 • www. hostalvirreyes.com.mx • $*

10 Hotel Metropol
This modern hotel offers spotlessly clean rooms decorated in neutral colors. The onsite restaurant serves Mexican entrées. 🕲 *Luis Moya 39, Col Centro • Map N3 • 1085-0830, 01-800-022-3099 • www.hotelmetropol.com. mx • No air conditioning • $*

Most hotels accept credit cards, but some mid-range and budget hotels expect cash

Price Categories

For a standard, double room per night (with breakfast if included), taxes, and extra charges.

$	under 1000 pesos
$$	1000–1500 pesos
$$$	1500–2000 pesos
$$$$	2000–2500 pesos
$$$$$	over 2500 pesos

Left **Hotel Condesa df** Right **Hotel La Casona**

🔟 Staying Around the City

Hotel Condesa df
Chic, modern, and casual, this boutique hotel is furnished in a classical yet contemporary style. The guestrooms are luxurious, simple, and tasteful with high ceilings and colorful handwoven rugs. The shady inner courtyard reminds you of an old hacienda, yet it is completely modern in ambience. ◈ Av Veracruz 102, Col Condesa • Map F4 • 5241-2600 • www. condesadf.com • $$$$

Hotel La Casona
With elegantly furnished rooms, this small and cozy, European-style hotel is housed in a former mansion with a stunning courtyard. The service is personal with a focus on comfort, privacy, and refined luxury. ◈ Durango 280, Col Roma • Map G4 • 5286-3001 • www.hotellacasona.com. mx • $$$

Stanza Hotel
This attractive multi-story hotel is located in the Roma area. The guestrooms are clean, comfortably sized, and come with carpeting and an in-room safe. The hotel has a business center, on-site restaurant, and a parking space. ◈ Av Álvaro Obregón 13, Col Roma • Map L5 • 5208-0052, 01-800-908-9600 • www.stanzahotel.com • Extra charge for rooms with air conditioning • $

Radisson Paraíso Perisur Hotel
This gleaming modern high-rise has a stunning and expansive atrium lobby with a fine Mexican restaurant. The rooms are spacious with large windows, contemporary furnishings, blue tone carpeting, well-lit desks, and in-room safes. ◈ Cúspide 53, Col Parques del Pedregal • 5927-5959, 1-800-395-7046 • www. radisson.com • $$$$

Casa de la Condesa
The rooms are clean with basic furnishings, and some of the rooms on the top floor face the park and have small balconies. Suites have larger rooms, small kitchenettes with microwave, and a small refrigerator. It is located in Roma near restaurants and cafés. ◈ Orizaba 16, Col Roma • Map K6 • 5584-3089 • www.casa delacondesa.net • $$

Hotel Roosevelt
This small modern hotel with 74 rooms is spotlessly clean, and the bilingual front-desk staff are very helpful. The guestrooms are pleasant and comfortable, with a small safe, Wi-Fi access, and cable TV. The hotel is located close to Condesa. ◈ Insurgentes Sur 287, Col Condesa • Map H5 • 5208-3606 • www.hotelroosevelt. mx • Air conditioning only in some rooms • $

Hilton Aeropuerto
This mid-sized modern hotel is located over the international terminal but it has excellent soundproofing. Some of the rooms look out over the airport runways. ◈ Benito Juárez International Airport • Map C2 • 5133-0500 • www.hilton.com • $$$

Crowne Plaza Hotel de México
This high-rise hotel near the World Trade Center has a dramatic two-story lobby with wood details and cozy seating areas. The rooms are large and have Jacuzzi tubs. ◈ Dakota 95, Col Nápoles • 1164-1164, 1-800-290-7906 • www.crowneplaza. com • $$$

Camino Real Aeropuerto
A high-rise hotel with large, attractive rooms. The business center is open 24 hours daily. ◈ Puerto México 80, Col Peñón de los Baños • Map C2 • 3003-0033 • www. caminoreal.com.mx • $$$$

El Patio 77
This converted private home, the city's first ecological B&B, is located in a residential area near many tourist sights. The rooms are attractively decorated with antiques and Mexican folk art. ◈ Icazbalceta 77, Col San Rafael • Map K1 • 5592-8452 • www. elpatio77.com • $$

General Index

Acknowledgments

The Author

Nancy Mikula's passion has been to explore America and discover its little-known attractions. Her articles on travel and history have appeared in numerous publications in the USA and Canada. She has authored Dorling Kindersley's Eyewitness Travel Top 10 guides to San Antonio & Austin and to Santa Fe. She also has collaborated on guides to Arizona, Southwest USA, and the Grand Canyon.

Main Photographer Paul Franklin
Additional Photography
Demetrio Carrasco, Rough Guides/ Alex Robinson, Peter Wilson, Linda Whitwam, Francesca Yorke, Begoña Zabalza, Michel Zabe.
Fact Checker Eva Gleason

At DK INDIA:

Managing Editor Aruna Ghose
Senior Editorial Manager Joseph Mathai
Design Manager Priyanka Thakur
Project Editor Souvik Mukherjee
Project Designer Mathew Kurien
Senior Cartographer Suresh Kumar
Cartographer Jasneet Kaur
Senior Picture Researcher Taiyaba Khatoon
Picture Research Assistance Sumita Khatwani

Indexer & Proofreader Pooja Kumari
Senior DTP Designer Vinod Harish

At DK LONDON:
Publisher Douglas Amrine
Publishing Manager Christine Stroyan
Design Manager Mabel Chan
Editors Hugh Thompson, Ros Walford
Designer Kate Leonard
Senior Cartographic Editor Casper Morris
DTP Designer Natasha Lu
Senior Picture Researcher Ellen Root
DK Picture Library Romaine Werblow, Myriam Meghrabi
Production Linda Dare
Revisions Editorial and Design
Emma Anacootee, Marta Bescos Sanchez, Emer FitzGerald, James Johnston, Claire Jones, Maite Lantaron, Nicola Malone, Alison McGill, Helen Partington, Sands Publishing Solutions, Conrad van Dyk

Picture Credits

a-above; b-below/bottom; c-centre; f-far; l-left; r-right; t-top.

The publishers would like to thank the following individuals, companies, and picture libraries for their kind permission to reproduce their photographs: Bar la Opera, Castillo de Chapultepec, Catedral Metropolitana, Embassy Suites, Hotel Cortés, Hotel Catedral, Italianni's, Los Danzantes, Museo Diego Rivera Anahuacalli, Museo Franz Mayer, Museo Nacional de Antropollogía, Museo Nacional de Arte, Museo Nacional de la Revolución, Palacio de Bellas Artes, Palacio Nacional, Plaza Florencia.

ALAMY IMAGES: Wendy Connett 104tl; Danita Delimont 38tr; Megapress 60cl; Mireille Vautier 76cr; Visual Arts Library (London) 39tl; Peter M. Wilson 89br.

THE ART ARCHIVE: Nicolas Sapieha 50t.

BLUE PURE LOYALTY: 87TL.

CORBIS: 39tr; Yann Arthus-Bertrand 103t; Bettmann 38tc; Sergio Dorantes 61clb; Free Agents Limited 36-7; JAI/Demetrio Carrasco 18-9; Gianni Dagli Orti 11bl.

GRAN HOTEL DE LA CIUDAD DE MÉXICO: 113tl.

THE GRANGER COLLECTION, New York: 38crb, 38tl.

HOTEL BRICK: 114tl.

HOTEL HABITA: 114tr

RESTAURANTE LES MOUSTACHES: 79tl.

TELMEX: 109tr.

Special Editions of DK Travel Guides

DK Travel Guides can be purchased in bulk quantities at discounted prices for use in promotions or as premiums. We are also able to offer special editions and personalized jackets, corporate imprints, and excerpts from all of our books, tailored specifically to meet your own needs.

To find out more, please contact:
(in the US) **SpecialSales@dk.com**
(in the UK) **TravelSpecialSales@uk.dk.com**
(in Canada) DK Special Sales at **general@tourmaline.ca**
(in Australia) **business.development@pearson.com.au**

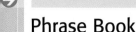

Phrase Book

In an Emergency

Help!	¡Socorro!	soh-**koh**-roh
Call a doctor!	¡Llame a un médico!	**yah**-meh ah **oon meh**-dee-koh
Call an ambulance!	¡Llame una ambulancia!	**yah**-meh ah ahm-boo-**lahn**-see-ah
Call the fire department!	¡Llame a los bomberos!	**yah**-meh ah lohs bohm-**beh**-rohs
policeman	el policía	ehl poh-lee-**see**-ah

Communication Essentials

Yes	Sí	see
No	No	noh
Please	Por favor	pohr fah-**vohr**
Thank you	Gracias	**grah**-see-ahs
Excuse me	Perdone	pehr-**doh**-neh
Hello	Hola	**oh**-lah
Bye (casual)	Chau	chau
Goodbye	Adiós	ah-dee-**ohs**
What?	¿Qué?	keh
When?	¿Cuándo?	**kwahn**-doh
Why?	¿Por qué?	pohr-**keh**
Where?	¿Dónde?	**dohn**-deh
How are you?	¿Cómo está usted?	**koh**-moh ehs-**tah** oos-**tehd**
Very well, thank you	Muy bien, gracias	mwee bee-**ehn grah**-see-ahs
I'm sorry	Lo siento	loh see-**ehn**-toh

Useful Phrases

Where is/are…?	¿Dónde está/están…?	**dohn**-deh ehs-**tah**/ehs-**tahn**
How far is it to…?	¿Cuántos metros/ kilómetros hay de aquí a…?	**kwahn**-tohs **meh**-trohs/kee-**loh**-meh-trohs **eye** deh ah-**kee** ah
Which way is it to…?	¿Por dónde se va a…?	pohr **dohn**-deh seh **vah** ah
Do you speak English?	¿Habla inglés?	**ah**-blah een-**glehs**
I don't understand	No comprendo	noh kohm-**prehn**-doh
I would like	Quisiera/ Me gustaría	kee-see-**yehr**-ah meh goo-stah-**ree** ah

Useful Words

big	grande	**grahn**-deh
small	pequeño/a	peh-**keh**-nyoh/nyah
hot	caliente	kah-lee-**ehn**-teh
cold	frío/a	**free**-oh/ah
good	bueno/a	**bweh**-noh/nah
bad	malo/a	**mah**-loh/lah
open	abierto/a	ah-bee-**ehr**-toh/tah
closed	cerrado/a	sehr-**rah**-doh/dah
left	izquierda	ees-key-**ehr**-dah
right	derecha	deh-**reh**-chah
(keep) straight ahead	(siga) derecho	(**see**-gah) deh-**reh**-choh
near	cerca	**sehr**-kah
far	lejos	**leh**-hohs
more	más	mahs
less	menos	**meh**-nohs
entrance	entrada	ehn-**trah**-dah
exit	salida	sah-**lee**-dah
elevator	el ascensor	ehl ah-sehn-**sohr**
toilets	baños/	**bah**-nyohs/

Post Offices and Banks

Where can I change money?	¿Dónde puedo cambiar dinero?	**dohn**-deh **pweh**-doh kahm-bee-**ahr** dee-**neh**-roh
How much is the postage to…?	¿Cuánto cuesta enviar una carta a…?	**kwahn**-toh **kweh**-stah ehn-vee-**yahr oo**-nah **kahr**-tah ah
I need stamps	Necesito estampillas	neh-seh-**see**-toh ehs-tahm-**pee**-yahs

Shopping

How much does this cost?	¿Cuánto cuesta esto?	**kwahn**-toh **kwehs**-tah ehs-toh
I would like…	Me gustaría…	meh goos-tah-**ree**-ah
Do you have?	¿Tienen?	tee-**yeh**-nehn
Do you take credit cards/ traveler's checks?	¿Aceptan tarjetas de crédito/ cheques de viajero?	ahk-**sehp**-tahn tahr-**heh**-tahs deh **kreh**-dee-toh/ **cheh**-kehs deh vee-ah-**heh**-roh
expensive	caro	**kahr**-oh
cheap	barato	bah-**rah**-toh
white	blanco	**blahn**-koh
black	negro	**neh**-groh
red	rojo	**roh**-hoh
yellow	amarillo	ah-mah-**ree**-yoh
green	verde	**vehr**-deh
blue	azul	ah-**sool**
bank	el banco	ehl **bahn**-koh
market	el tianguis/ mercado	ehl tee-ahn-goo-ees/mehr-**kah**-doh
post office	la oficina de correos	lah oh-fee-**see**-nah deh kohr-**reh**-ohs
supermarket	el supermercado	ehl soo-pehr-mehr-**kah**-doh
travel agency	la agencia de viajes	lah ah-**hehn**-see-ah deh vee-**ah**-hehs

Transportation

When does the… leave?	¿A qué hora sale el…?	ah **keh oh**-rah **sah**-leh ehl
Where is bus stop?	¿Dónde está la parada de camiones?	**dohn**-deh ehs-**tah** lah pah-**rah**-dah deh kah-mee-**ohn**-es
Is there a bus /train to…?	¿Hay un camión/ tren a…?	**eye** oon kah-mee-**ohn**/**trehn** ah
ticket office	la taquilla	lah tah-**kee**-yah
round-trip ticket	un boleto de ida y vuelta	oon boh-**leh**-toh deh **ee**-dah ee voo-**ehl**-tah
one-way ticket	un boleto de ida solamente	oon boh-**leh**-toh deh **ee**-dah soh-lah-**mehn**-teh
airport	el aeropuerto	ehl ah-ehr-oh-poo-

Sightseeing

museum	el museo	ehl moo-**seh**-oh
cathedral	la catedral	lah kah-teh-**drahl**

church	la iglesia/ la basílica	lah ee-**gleh**-see-ah/ lah bah-**see**-lee-kah
garden	el jardín	ehl hahr-**deen**
pyramid	la pirámide	lah pee-**rah**-meed
tourist information office	la oficina de turismo	lah oh-fee-**see**-nah deh too-**rees**-moh
ticket	la entrada	lah ehn-**trah**-dah
guide (person)	el/la guía	ehl/lah **gee**-ah
guide (book)	la guía	lah **gee**-ah
map	el mapa	ehl **mah**-pah
taxi stand	sitio de taxis	**see**-tee-oh deh **tahk**-sees

Staying in a Hotel

Do you have a vacant room?	¿Tienen una habitación libre?	tee-**eh**-nehn **oo**-nah ah-bee-tah-see-**ohn lee**-breh
double room	habitación doble	ah-bee-tah-see-**ohn doh**-bleh
single room	habitación sencilla	ah-bee-tah-see-**ohn** sehn-**see**-yah
room with a bath	habitación con baño	ah-bee-tah-see-**ohn** kohn **bah**-nyoh
shower	la ducha	lah **doo**-chah
I have a reservation	Tengo una habitación reservada	tehn-goh **oo**-nah ah-bee-tah-see-**ohn** reh-sehr-**vah**-dah
key	la llave	lah **yah**-veh

Eating Out

Have you got a table for…	¿Tienen mesa para…?	tee-**eh**-nehn meh-sah pah-**rah**
I want to reserve a table	Quiero reservar una mesa	kee-eh-roh reh-sehr-**vahr oo**-nah **meh**-sah
The bill, please	La cuenta, por favor	lah **kwehn**-tah, pohr fah-**vohr**
I am a vegetarian	Soy vegetariano/a	soy veh-heh-tah-ree-**ah**-no/na
waiter/waitress	mesero/a	meh-**seh**-roh/rah
menu	la carta	lah **kahr**-tah
wine list	la carta de vinos	lah **kahr**-tah deh **vee**-nohs
glass	un vaso	oon **vah**-soh
knife	un cuchillo	oon koo-**chee**-yoh
fork	un tenedor	oon teh-neh-**dohr**
spoon	una cuchara	oo-nah koo-**chah**-rah
breakfast	el desayuno	ehl deh-sah-**yoo**-noh
lunch	la comida	lah koh-**mee**-dah
dinner	la cena	lah **seh**-nah
main course	el plato fuerte	ehl **plah**-toh foo-**ehr**-teh
starters	las entradas	lahs ehn-**trah**-das

Menu Decoder

el aceite	ah-**see-eh**-teh	oil
las aceitunas	ah-seh-**toon**-ahs	olives
el agua mineral	**ah**-gwa mee-neh-**rahl**	mineral water
el ajo	**ah**-hoh	garlic
el arroz	ahr-**rohs**	rice
el azúcar	ah-**soo**-kahr	sugar
una bebida	beh-**bee**-dah	drink
el café	kah-**feh**	coffee
la carne	**kahr**-neh	meat
la cebolla	seh-**boh**-yah	onion
la cerveza	sehr-**veh**-sah	beer
el cerdo	sehr-doh	pork
el chocolate	choh-koh-**lah**-teh	chocolate
la ensalada	ehn-sah-**lah**-dah	salad
la fruta	froo-tah	fruit
el helado	eh-**lah**-doh	ice cream
el huevo	oo-**eh**-voh	egg
el jugo	ehl **hoo**-goh	juice
la langosta	lahn-**gohs**-tah	lobster
la leche	**leh**-cheh	milk
la mantequilla	mahn-teh-**kee**-yah	butter
los mariscos	mah-**rees**-kohs	seafood
el pan	pahn	bread
el pescado	pehs-**kah**-doh	fish
picante	pee-**kahn**-teh	spicy
la pimienta	pee-mee-**yehn**-tah	pepper
el pollo	**poh**-yoh	chicken
el postre	**pohs**-treh	dessert
el queso	**keh**-soh	cheese
el refresco	reh-**frehs**-koh	soft drink/soda
la sal	sahl	salt
la salsa	**sahl**-sah	sauce
la sopa	**soh**-pah	soup
el té	teh	herb tea (usually camomile)
el té negro	teh neh-groh	tea
la torta	**tohr**-tah	sandwich
las tostadas	tohs-**tah**-dahs	toast
el vinagre	vee-**nah**-greh	vinegar
el vino blanco	**vee**-noh **blahn**-koh	white wine
el vino tinto	**vee**-noh **teen**-toh	red wine

Numbers

0	cero	**seh**-roh
1	uno	**oo**-noh
2	dos	dohs
3	tres	trehs
4	cuatro	**kwa**-troh
5	cinco	**seen**-koh
6	seis	says
7	siete	**see**-eh-teh
8	ocho	**oh**-choh
9	nueve	**nweh**-veh
10	diez	dee-**ehs**
20	veinte	**veh**-een-teh
30	treinta	**treh**-een-tah
40	cuarenta	kwah-**rehn**-tah
50	cincuenta	seen-**kwehn**-tah
60	sesenta	seh-**sehn**-tah
70	setenta	seh-**tehn**-tah
80	ochenta	oh-**chehn**-tah
90	noventa	noh-**vehn**-tah
100	cien	see-**ehn**
200	doscientos	dohs-see-**ehn**-tohs
500	quinientos	khee-nee-**ehn**-tohs
1,000	mil	meel

Time

one minute	un minuto	oon mee-**noo**-toh
one hour	una hora	**oo**-nah **oh**-rah
half an hour	media hora	meh-dee-ah **oh**-rah
Monday	lunes	**loo**-nehs
Tuesday	martes	**mahr**-tehs
Wednesday	miércoles	mee-**ehr**-koh-lehs
Thursday	jueves	hoo-**weh**-vehs
Friday	viernes	vee-**ehr**-nehs
Saturday	sábado	**sah**-bah-doh
Sunday	domingo	doh-**meen**-goh

Bold letters in the pronunciation guides indicate the stressed syllable

Selected Street Index

Selected Street Index